Galactic Human
Handbook

Entering
The New Time
Creating Planetary Groups

Sheldon Nidle & José Argüelles

ALTEA

ISBN 0 9524555 5 2

British Library Cataloguing-in-Publication Data. A catalogue record
for this book is available from the British Library.

Cover illustration: *Bridge of Angels* copyright © Mark Mironov
Layout and setting by Altea Publishing
Printed by Guernsey Press Ltd
Published in 1995 by Altea Publishing, Parkmount House,
10 St Leonards Road, Forres IV36 0DW, Scotland

Contents

Part One
Galactic Human Handbook: Creating Planetary Advocate Groups

Part Two
Entering the New Time
Creation of Planetary Calendar Councils and a Planet Art Network

Appendix
VictoryNet/Operation Victory Resources

Video tapes, audio tapes, books, software

VictoryNet Round Table

VictoryNet Websites

Galactic Human Handbook

Creating Planetary Advocate Groups

Sheldon Nidle

Illustrations by Miriam de Vera Nidle

Acknowledgements

Every book has a number of highly dedicated people that have made it possible for it to be created — including this book. My deepest thanks and acknowledgement goes to Katherine Lauster for giving her time to transcribe lecture number nine on Planetary Advocate Groups that served as the basis for this work. My deepest acknowledgements and deepest loving thanks also go to Vita and Sandra at Altea Publishing whose editing and contribution of the costs of publication truly made this work possible. Also my sincerest thanks go to Paradise Newland for her thoughtful sculpting of this book and especially to my former wife, Miriam de Vera Nidle, whose illustrations and computer expertise got me through some difficult times.

And to Dr. Rob Schweder, Valerie Donner, and all the crew at Operation Victory whose support and guidance has helped to make possible this final edition that you are now reading. Finally my thanks go to all the great brother and sister Light workers whose silent, yet mighty, efforts have allowed this work to go forth into the world and be applied. Thanks also to Washta, the Ascended Masters of Sirius and Earth, and to the Spiritual Hierarchy. Let it be known that Spirit's miraculous work has been done!

Lastly, my deep thanks and gratitude goes to José and Lloydine Argüelles whose contribution to this book of their materials on galactic time have greatly added to the necessary information included in this work. Also my many thanks to Elizabeth Whitney and to all 'Time Bandits' everywhere for their assistance in helping to make possible the new age of galactic time.

Dedication

*This book is lovingly dedicated to my son, Narturi.
Just know that your father loves you very, very much.*

Introduction

The purpose of this text is to inform the reader of the importance of Planetary Advocate Groups and how to form them. For many years, there have existed individuals on this planet who have used their energies and abilities to aid *Gaia* — the great Earth Mother — and their fellow humanity. Now a time has come for a new beginning that will add to the work accomplished by these bright souls. It is a time for the bringing together of Earth's humanity. Moreover, it is also a time for realizing how we are all connected to one another.

We are living in an age that is noted for the spread of an electronic technology that has made possible instantaneous worldwide communications. This seemingly miraculous ability to communicate instantly with one another has opened up a new era of information that has tied together the Earth's human populations in a new way. This is the first time in human history that an era has existed that could allow such a pertinent witness to the world's events as this one. We can see the daily dramas of human and planetary existence being deftly played out before us. We are now both observers and players in these cosmic dramas that deeply affect us all.

This planetary age is indeed a period of immediate communications and with it a vast accumulation of data has become possible. At this time, you and I are on the verge of being uplifted into this exploding sea of worldwide information. Yet, this vast increase in data and knowledge has given us a distinct advantage. We now have at our finger tips the very pulse of our planet, our civilization and our universe. This explosion of knowledge has also made possible a means to explore and to begin to understand what goes on around us, which in turn has led to a growth in the search for reality and the reasons for human consciousness. More and more Earth humans are attempting to discover the nature of who and what they are. This search has led this era of human history to be an age of communications and data networks as well as an age of a great inner exploration of what constitutes human consciousness.

In contrast to previous times, the current search for what creates human existence involves more than just a few intelligentsia and their rich supporters; it involves all of Earth's humanity. This search signifies a vast shift in how humans perceive not only themselves, but also their planet. It is a search that is bringing humans closer to the original meanings of universal creation, something that has not been possible since the wondrous age of the prophets and the patriarchs of biblical times. As we all search for these hidden truths, we become needful of those persons who can give us clues and directions to the path of consciousness which we all seek. This map that we are looking for may seem difficult to find. Yet it is not as difficult a task as it would at first appear.

The key to this search lies in the recent events of this century. Since the end of World War II, there has been a rise in consciousness that has coincided with a concern for the Earth. The first stage of this development was the slow rise of the environmental movement in the early 1950s which culminated with its ascent into prominence in the 1970s. This movement was paralleled by an increase in consciousness groups that explored the need for meditation and its use to calm the proliferating negative energy of modern human civilization. It was only a matter of time before these diverse movements would begin to discover a way to merge their efforts.

Simultaneously, there appeared in the media of the post-World-War-II era a new and strange phenomenon — the so-called 'flying saucer' or UFO. Its message was, initially, one of harmony given by humanoid space beings from other worlds. This concept of UFO-nauts has become more varied since the humanoid contacts in the early 1950s and 1960s. However, it is still a message of great importance to planet Earth that is now being reiterated by myself and others. The significance of this message is that it can give Earth humans a way to bridge our own social technology and the social technology of the extraterrestrials for the development of new core groups to aid our civilization through its present transitions.

In addition, the Spiritual Hierarchy has made humans more aware of their existence. This development was created by the diffusion through the media of accounts of what can be called 'near death experiences'. Such experiences have allowed people to read and view compelling evidence of the fact that all humans exist within a reality that is much greater than themselves. Such significant messages with references to a group of protectors and helpers (angels) has opened up an even greater awareness among humans of the need to reassess human consciousness. This new evaluation of human spirituality by Earth's humanity has led to the need to discover how this new-found spirituality should influence our daily lives.

The advent of a new perception about spirituality has also led to the end of the secrecy placed around the ancient wisdoms of the Earth's indigenous peoples. This recent development has allowed the tribal shamans to come forward with their varied and powerful message. That important message is part of the remarkable mix of information which has been made possible by this civilization's amazing electronic technology.

These various factors — the environmental movement, the new perceptions about spirituality, the wisdom of the indigenous peoples, and the re-emerging extraterrestrial message — have come together to create the need for a new movement that could encase their vast diversities and allow for a way that could unite all of them into a single cause. This cause could then act as the foundation for a new and more dynamic human civilization — a human civilization that is both planetary and galactic in scope. This mounting need has led to the requirement for a new and more dynamic organization that could serve as the foundation for the now emerging galactic civilization.

One may indeed ask what are the requirements for a human civilization to be considered galactic? First, a galactic civilization is a civilization that has learned that it is part of an interconnected whole called the galactic life net. Such a civilization realizes that it is primarily responsible for the biosphere of planet Earth. It is more than just environmentally oriented in its policy decisions. A galactic civilization understands that the Earth is a living being and that we humans are its stewards or guardians. Our responsibility is to be true and respectful guests and to abide by the rules given us by *Gaia's* angelic hosts. Second, a galactic civilization is a civilization that uses its technology to aid this planet and to enhance the lives of all beings who dwell on it. To do so, Earth human technology, as amazing as it now seems, has to be made more user- and life-friendly. This process means that our planetary civilization's economy and its government will have to be vastly altered from its present form. Our planetary economy should be reformed from one based on scarcity and allowable levels of pollution to a galactic one based on abundance and Earth-friendliness. This concept is possible due to new emerging and previously suppressed technologies and economic devices that can quickly alter the nature of our contemporary society. Finally, a galactic civilization is a civilization that honors and respects its vast and ancient roots. It understands the wondrousness of its historical development and how the past, present and future have been blended together to produce a truly unique creation — galactic human civilization and divine right order acting as one.

Besides all of these wonderful things that a galactic civilization represents, it is also a vehicle that is designed to hold the full consciousness of galactic humans and direct them into meaningful purposes. This ability comes from the use of what I call 'fluid management'. It is a technique that allows for humans to be able to both express their potentials and to make an important contribution to their civilization. As we explore the meanings and directions of advocacy, let us realize that it is necessary first to redesign the whole concept of what constitutes organizational procedures. We as a species are moving from a concept of a planetary human to that of a galactic human. Hence, we are also moving from organizational structures based on competition to ones based on creation. Creation allows that humans be able to participate in groups at levels that encourage them to make meaningful contributions to their group. These new concepts of organization allow for temporary alteration of the group's leadership according to the gifts of each of its members.

In this way, we see galactic human civilization as a series of fluid parts that move or 'flow' according to the needs of the society and most importantly to the requirements of the universe. This concept of 'flow' is another dynamic element in the mix. Time takes on a new and vital dimension. It is the regulator of what we might today call divine law and order. The Angelic Realms become the givers of a special element — right order. This divine order or energy of creation is regulated in the physical by the Time Lords and is given to galactic humans by the Time Keepers. In our initial organizations, the Time Keepers will have to be substituted by the use of a group concept arrived at by means to be discussed later in this book.

My hope is that the unique organization to be described in this book will rapidly spread across this planet. It has the ability to become the foundation for a unique type of civilization newly arising on this planet. For we are all a unique embodiment of humanity. Let us use this embodiment and combine it with full consciousness to create a new type of galactic civilization that can truly show its third-dimensional mastery and its love of self-determination.

Joyfully,

Sheldon Nidle

ONE

Definition of a Planetary Advocate Group

Let us begin this discussion of Planetary Advocate Groups with both a general and a more specific description of the form they are to take. Furthermore, let us look at how they are able to create the positive energies that are needed to establish a galactic civilization.

Planetary Advocate Groups — What are they?

On Sirius and in other galactic human civilizations, there is inculcated into every human a spirit of self-worth and great inner spiritual strength based on the need for personal sovereignty. This spirit of personal sovereignty is now beginning to take hold once again on this planet we call Earth. One of the major ways in which it will be directly expressed is through the formation of what I call Planetary Advocate Groups (PAGs). These groups can be roughly defined as spiritually committed advocates for *Gaia* (Mother Earth) and for the rapid evolution of human culture from a presently limited consciousness to a full galactic one.

That is, Planetary Advocate Groups are the informed and highly trusted champions of the Earth's environment (*Gaia*'s physical essence) — and also of those indigenous human cultures and their sacred traditions (those who understand *Gaia*'s spiritual essence) that aid this planetary advocacy.

Planetary Advocate Groups can be divided into two types. Firstly, there are those groups which are primarily devoted to working with the Spiritual Hierarchy (more on these and their role in Chapter 2 on Guardian groups) and secondly there are the groups who are devoted advocates of Mother Gaia and of the indigenous peoples and their rituals and culture. In addition, both are the conveyers of the knowledge and the means to raise humanity's consciousness. By so doing, these groups will use their ability to help humans learn the many forms that can be applied to discover the path to full consciousness.

Advocacy is both a spiritual quest and a moral one; moreover, it is also a formula to return each Earth human to their inner soul purpose. These developments have brought us to this particular time and especially to this specific place — this magnificent living ball of mud that we call Mother Earth. They have also brought us to this present period of evolutionary change in Earth human culture and civilization. The times that we live in are ones set for a new American and a new planetary revolution.

PAGs — An historical perspective

This worldwide revolution is not to be primarily of a political nature, but a great moral and spiritual one. We now sit on the brink of a developing new age of spirituality which has the ability to catapult our civilization into a whole new set of realities. We have briefly touched upon this in the book *First Contact: Birthing a Galactic Civilization* (to be published 1995/6) and we would now wish to expound upon it again in a new and quite different manner.

To do so, let us move from *First Contact*"s overall explanations of the forthcoming great shifts in consciousness and reality into considering how we can best help these changes come about. For, as they happen, these changes affect both the Earth's and our own realities. What I wish to do in this short book is to go into the specifics as much as is possible and to use this knowledge given to me by the Spiritual Hierarchy and the Galactic Federation to help you, dear readers, to dedicate yourselves to assisting this process of consciousness change. So let us consider what these groups are and what they truly represent.

The first thing that I want to explain in some depth is why we need Planetary Advocate Groups. This will include learning what these groups are — a point that we shall also be discussing in greater detail during the course of this book. However, let us start with a key point that involves their importance to the whole scenario of consciousness change.

The past few decades have given rise to a number of groups which, each in their own way, have attempted to hold the focus for change. These groups sat at the core of what is right and what is wrong with how change is effected in our society. There have been various environmental and/or spiritual groups or organizations which have attempted in their own unique and wonderful ways to bring together the energies of both the Spiritual Hierarchy and the new environmental consciousness that is now rapidly developing on this planet for the purpose of facilitating certain policies and explaining important concepts.

PAGs — *Their structure and 'fluid management'*

These organizations formulated ideas that would allow people to better understand how this planet's ecological and spiritual systems operate and how human society can bring about this change in consciousness. Yet they lacked a clear and flexible form of organization and an easily accessible media in which to explain their purpose.

We have now reached a time when a newer and more integrated group is to be formed — and this is what I am calling the Planetary Advocate Group. These groups will be organizations that combine all of the previously mentioned concepts in a different and more proficient way. Such an organizational concept will allow advocate groups to be all that these other groups have yet to be.

However, given the self-imposed limitations of these original groups, they have done a wonderful job of bringing in all the strengths of the Christ energies, and the supreme energies of God and the Spiritual Hierarchy (more about these Guardian groups in the next chapter). These environmental and spiritual groups have also allowed people to learn about and experience the nature of Mother Earth — what Earth's nurturing energies are about — and the need to achieve balance by moving away from a paternalistic society toward a more maternalistic one.

Such organizations have been pertinent for their own time and for their own purposes — in other words, they have gotten the job done up to now. However, I want to emphasize that the importance of the new Planetary Advocate Groups that we are now discussing is that they embody not only a new method of organizing these older types of groups (utilizing *fluid management* — see Chapters 4 and 5) but also a new way of understanding the energies of the universe and how it relates to humans (the concept of self-sovereignty). It is the responsibility of the Planetary Advocate Groups to integrate this knowledge into our developing human planetary civilization.

This communication and networking responsibility is a very important point which must be emphasized. We have moved from an age in which there was an exclusivity about perceived reality to one in which everyone thought that if they got together and did their own thing in a certain way it would bring about change. Now we are in a new period in which another element must be added. We have entered an era of interconnectedness. This interconnection involves the coming together of all living things on our planet.

In effect, we are now feeling the need to connect with ourselves and with others on as deep a level as is humanly possible. In this regard, there is interconnection developing between the spiritual and physical energies of this planet as well as with the organizations of our space brothers and sisters (the Galactic Federation), and the various hierarchical organizations that Spirit has brought forth to help physical creation achieve its full light. All these various aspects have now come together in and around our planet in order to aid its growth towards full consciousness.

Basically, these pieces of our puzzle have been revealed to Earth humans over the last few thousand years. The important point to be made here is that during the last two decades a number of great events have occurred that have allowed people to begin to see the importance of Spirit in human society and in the entire concept of human development — the principles under which human societies operate.

We need a new form of governance

Governments are being told they have to change because they are no longer relevant. The reasons why they are no longer relevant are twofold. First of all, they fail to provide us with the programs we require to correctly utilize our physical, social, economic and spiritual resources. Secondly, they fail to provide the spiritual underpinnings that would justify their given authority.

So we have to develop a new concept of government and also a new idea of how people within a particular society would relate to this form of highly conscious and spiritual government. This new range of relationships that we are now developing is based on a

re-spiritualization, as I would like to call it, of the concept of government and also a re-spiritualization of the way in which humans
conduct their lives with one another in an ever-changing planetary
society.

It is this key factor which I would now like to talk about and
describe its various aspects in greater detail. So let us begin by going
into a fuller description of Planetary Advocate Groups.

The importance of PAGs

We have already said that the importance of these groups lies in
the fact that they do things in a newer and more effective way. This
approach allows the various spiritual and intellectual aspects, to
which we have already alluded, to interlink more easily and thereby to infuse into the ever-increasing planetary consciousness.

Such groups will also permit a much greater degree of participation from those people who up till now have not belonged to
meditation groups or taken part in groups that have aided Earth's
sovereignty. This lack of involvement was due to a belief held by
the majority of the Earth's human population that this was not how
things were supposed to be done. Further, they also felt that this
was the wrong moment in time to bring change to our planet and
its human civilization. However, a new consciousness has descend-
ed upon everyone on this planet and they are now looking for a
truly acceptable way of applying their newly found realities. So let
us look at these various aspects that we have just mentioned and
continue from there.

First of all, Planetary Advocate Groups will simply consist of
light workers, and I am going to define a light worker here as *any
human being who has within them a deep, positive spiritual feeling to do
something that gives them great joy and helps the planet and our human
culture to become more conscious.* This rising consciousness can later
be amplified through an actual inner voice or 'conscience' which
may externalise as an angelic guardian.

An angelic guardian is a special spirit which guides a person,
or in fact attempts to encourage a form of meditation or quiet prayer.
This inner time is important, for it helps us to understand the basic
principles of what we are now in the midst of. That is why I call us

light workers — because we are dealing with the awesome energy of spiritual light.

So initially these groups will consist of light workers who have come together to help restore the planet and to help restore ourselves. This is the first major aspect of consciousness that most humans are picking up in our society — the concept that our planet, Mother Earth, must be restored, as well as us ourselves.

Some people may view the planet as a living being, as I do. Others may see it just as an object that we dwell upon but which now has to be developed in a much saner way. This conscious change has led many to re-evaluate their integrity and their ability to live within present Earth human civilization.

Whether people hold the first view or the second or a combination of both, the key point is that the first major spiritual inspiration many people receive is to restore the planet as well as themselves. These messages come in many forms whether as predictions from scientific and environmental experts, or as prophecies from biblical or other ancient spiritual sources, for example Lord Michael. These prophecies always emphasise the importance of humans restoring the planet, restoring the great Earth Mother, and this is the key reason for creating advocate groups.

PAGs — *some key concepts*

I call these groups Planetary Advocate Groups because their primary purpose is to act as advocates — or in other words, champions — for the planet. They are designed to act in a way that helps all of us to truly understand what the planet and their role of planetary restoration is all about — i.e. the planet's energy pattern, et cetera.

Secondly, I have been given an organizational process that I call *fluid management*. These various groups have to show how we can be successfully governed by the principles of *fluid management*. This innovative approach is a new notion of the way a group's dynamics can be put together.

We shall discuss this concept in greater detail later on in this book (see Chapter 5: Fluid Management). Here we will give just a basic series of examples to explain it. Overall, *fluid management* is simply a way of allowing groups to be flexible enough to handle a given situation or a particular task that they have to perform.

PAGs are to be set up in such a way that those of its members who see a need to perform a particular task or project, and who also understand the context of that project, can come to the fore and use their expertise to lead the group to a successful resolution of the task or situation.

Moreover, as the situation or project undergoes slight changes in its scope or goals, other members of the group can come forward and take their place as appropriate. Thus, management continually remains fluid, and that is why I have called it *fluid management*. It is important to note that the key to it is to be open about everyone and to allow the group situation to flow creatively (more about this in Chapter 5).

Finally, a Planetary Advocate Group is a group that educates and informs our society about the great changes in planetary and personal consciousness that are now occurring. It is important that these groups are established for restoring the planet. They also have to understand what is happening to planet Earth and to the energies around her. Planetary Advocate Groups have to have a deep understanding of how these changes in consciousness relate to themselves and to the energies of the planet.

In other words, there is a synchronicity between what they are and what planet Earth is. As a result, they will use the information they are given in order to understand the whole process of the enormous alteration in consciousness and light going on within this Solar system and the entire Milky Way Galaxy. Another important aspect is having the spiritual insight to realise our interconnectedness as spiritual brothers and sisters involved in the uniquely complex process of preparing our Earth human culture for full conscious galactic civilization.

So, to reiterate, these various activities are a key to the preparations needed for understanding our lovely blue planet Earth and the spiritual energies that surround her. Every person has to deeply understand this profound development and see how it relates to themselves, and how it also relates to the energies of the planet. PAGs will use the information that they are given to understand the entire process of conscious change and the accompanying vast reality shift.

Another important point concerns the spiritual element itself, which is based on the connection of all spiritual brothers and sisters involved in creating these planetary organizations. We have to realize that we have come together to help to re-create the spiritual essence of togetherness that was lost during the individualization (alienation) process of modern industrial society. Humans are gregarious beings who require an extended family for their support and to reassure them of their inner purpose.

PAGs will help to expedite the re-creation of these extended families for the purpose of transitioning Earth humans through their presently highly fragmented and dysfunctional societies into a planetary society and finally a galactic one. This rapid evolution is a vital key to preparing our Earth human society for the coming mass landings, for participation in building our galactic civilization, and especially for membership in the Galactic Federation.

What is the Galactic Federation?

For those who don't know what the Galactic Federation is, let me give you a definition. The Galactic Federation is *a group of planets and vast star systems and star leagues that are moving our galaxy into the light.*

They are a messenger group that is bringing into fruition the energies of the Spiritual Hierarchy and their messages of light for their great divine plan — in other words, they are acting as physical heavenly aids.

This is one aspect of what I call the three-pronged energies for restoring our true Earthly guardianship. These elements include the Spiritual Hierarchy, our own particular energy and soul purposes along with those provided by our groups, and the restoring and teaching energies of the cetaceans (whales and dolphins). Finally there is the loving assistance of the Galactic Federation itself.

PAGs — how do they operate?

So how do these groups operate? They use meditation practices as well as what I call effective networking and liaison. Using the principles of *fluid management* they link together different groups, by providing from within themselves teams whose job is to interact continually with other groups, by networking and advertising their purposes and abilities. They may liaise with many other kinds of groups — such as a Guardian group which they may be inviting in to help them, or an environmental group, or a group whose sole purpose is working with the spiritual energies of the planet, et cetera.

All of these different types of groups are going to be brought together through appropriate information and by explaining to the community what the advocate group's mission is. In addition, PAGs will be showing other groups how they can interlink with them and work to provide for any particular group's own purposes as well as the purposes of the Planetary Advocate Group itself.

Finally, PAGs exist to make sure that what I call the divine light of order and the divine plan of our Spiritual Hierarchy is followed. The way that this task will be accomplished will involve all the different advocate groups on this planet coming together and interacting among themselves in as creative a way as possible. These types of interaction will become possible due to special worldwide computer networks and the formation of Life/Light Centers on a worldwide basis.

When the PAGs interlink, they are going to create tremendous light energies which will represent the visions of the various segments of the Spiritual Hierarchy — many Angels and Archangels will be visiting and giving visions to direct the whole process of conscious change.

Summary

As we have seen, PAGs are a unique way to bring together the various light workers of this planet. In so doing, PAGs will act as the framework around which to creatively and dynamically establish the various principles of the new developing human and planetary consciousness.

In this chapter I have given a very basic and simplistic explanation of what Planetary Advocate Groups are. Before looking at how to create such groups, let us review the nature and purpose of Guardian groups.

Two

Guardian Groups and Their Importance

As we look at the long history of spiritual groups, we see that many have had a great tradition of secrecy. This practice arose from the necessity of maintaining a knowledge that was too powerful to become public. For many years, the true intent of a Guardian group's spiritual endeavors was to do the 'work' in as quiet an environment as possible.

Reasons for secrecy and training

They believed that to do spiritual work properly required a great deal of initial preparation and training — which usually consisted of attaining proficiency in a specific type of meditation practice and a number of rather esoteric forms of knowledge. Each group guarded its inner secrets because they had two great fears.

First, they were afraid that their knowledge would be misused by those who were of the wrong temperament. This conviction was based on the fact that many persons who were not yet ready to properly apply this special knowledge had greatly misused it.

Second, they feared that exposure of the group's purposes and knowledge would lead to ridicule and make it much more difficult for them to complete their assigned tasks.

The wonder of their endeavors

We should be in awe of the great tasks that these groups have performed in their quiet manner. For each of them has been a keeper of the flame of higher consciousness and their special teachings have kept alive the great Western esoteric tradition.

From the beginning of the 19th century to the eighth decade of this century, their work has allowed for the setting of a spiritual energy that has permitted our present generation to reap the benefits of a rising new consciousness. Their great work has now led to the eventual ascension of both this planet and our civilization.

Among their activities have been the meditations that have helped to heal our planet and the procedures that have aided the Angels and the Ascended Masters in their vital tasks of administering to the needs of humanity and Mother Earth's life-giving sphere.

These tasks were conducted with little publicity or public knowledge, due to the belief that the public was not ready for what these groups had to offer. In their terminology, the public had too little consciousness to understand what they were attempting to accomplish.

A brief history of Guardian groups

The first groups were formed as a means to quietly do the work that had been started by the great eternal Masters who have visited this planet from time to time. During the course of the 19th century, several of these Masters began to visit various individuals and asked them to form groups to continue their Master's own work on this physical plane.

These groups were created all over Europe, Asia, Africa, Australia and the Americas. Each one dedicated itself to the work either of one particular Ascended Master or of a number of them. By the late 19th century, these groups had begun to set the energy for a new consciousness on the planet. The result was the rise of the first great series of spiritual organizations that put many of the ideas given to these Guardian groups into the public eye.

By the turn of the century, these newer and more public spiritual groups had amassed an international following and set the stage for the new series of meditation and/or ritual groups that would form in the period before the outbreak of the First World War. This new generation of spiritual groups was different from those formed in the previous century because they believed in a more public demeanor to their work. As a result, the population of Western Europe was exposed to the meanings of their ancient pre-Christian rituals and was allowed to begin to see the relationships between these rituals and those espoused by the Christian church.

This practice of various European Guardian groups helped to bring many converts to the spiritual movement and permitted a lot of the previously unknown esoteric knowledge to become open to public scrutiny. Such openness led to a grand series of discussions between the great lights of the Guardian movement, but it also exposed many individuals to a lot of public ridicule.

The outcome of this activity was that the groups involved with safeguarding much of this important esoteric knowledge became even more protective of their identity during the period of the first great war (1914-1918). By the end of the war, they had become highly fragmented and secretive and they returned to their previous position of self-containment.

This behavior led many Guardian groups to operate on two levels — an outer level that still appeared somewhat open and a more secretive inner circle (where the esoteric knowledge was kept) that required a great number of initiations in order to become a trusted member. By the end of the decade these inner circles had grown to be quite exclusive in their membership. The door had again swung shut on the great majority of Earth's humanity. The time for the disclosure of this material was to come later.

In the 1920s and the early 1930s, these groups became further divided by the advent of many social movements which had taken some of the esoteric materials partially disclosed by the Guardians and were using it for their own purposes. This development further fortified the belief of the Guardian groups' inner circles that this knowledge could only be given with a great deal of previous training.

Such a belief led many members of the inner circles of the Guardian groups to form their own small meditation groups in the hope that they could discover those individuals who were best suited for the training necessary before the great knowledge could be passed on. At the same time, the Ascended Masters had decided that the energy of love had to be given to the planet in a slightly different manner.

So, in the late 1930s, the Councils of the Ascended Masters began to surface in the channeled messages of many psychics around the world and to give forth assurances of hope and of joy. Their purpose was to open up the now closed channels to their knowledge by creating a number of public movements that would attract the attention of the mass public. This energy created a series of movements worldwide that helped to establish the anchor points for the light and move the Guardian groups into new directions.

These new directions began to become more evident when many of these Guardian groups began to advocate a more public-oriented disclosure of their materials. There was also an increase in channeled materials in the late 1930s. This development was the source for more open disclosures of the ancient knowledge by the end of this decade. However the outbreak of World War II in 1939 put an end to the environment necessary for such disclosures to continue.

The war years saw a return to the secrecy of earlier times, but deep in the Guardian movement the first messages were being given that this planet was approaching a time of great decision and that it was necessary to become more open with the materials that each of these groups had long guarded. Such messages led many groups to change their attitudes back to those of the late 1930s and the result was a great increase in the number of people attracted to the groups during the late 1940s.

At the same time, a new element was added to the mix. Many of the early ET contactees began to embrace a philosophy that proved to be very similar to the messages given by the Ascended Masters during the late 1930s.

This combination of the messages of the ET contactees and the direction now being followed by many Guardian groups led them into direct conflict over the validity of their respective messages. This series of difficulties caused many Guardian groups to denounce the contactees and create a wide rift between the two. The dispute has lasted for the past few decades and at times has threatened the unity of the spiritual movement. It is now time for this wide rift to be healed so that everyone can truly understand the importance of what is presently occurring.

During the decades following the end of the Second World War, we have entered a new era for the Guardian groups and their great traditions. They are now beginning to feel the need to cooperate more with those organizations and institutions that have been created since the late 1930s. These groups realized from the beginning that the 'work' had to become a more public-oriented endeavor. They also knew that the profound esoteric message had to be delivered in manner that would be easily assimilated by ordinary people.

This approach has led to a great number of public events and mass publications and has allowed the new consciousness to begin to make itself known in the last two decades. As this movement grows in numbers and success, it has put a lot of pressure on the Guardian groups and their tradition of secrecy.

New realities and Guardian groups

It is this great tradition that is now being re-evaluated by the various Guardian groups and many of them are changing direction completely and endorsing our attempt to aid in the restoration of full consciousness to our planet and our human civilization. This development is indeed welcomed by myself and by all concerned.

For all of us are now involved in this wondrous endeavor. Spirit has been able to work a marvelous turnabout and to present us with some wonderful teachers. Many of them have been involved with knowledge that allows us to gain a full understanding of the great changes that are now occurring all around us.

We should allow such teachers to instruct us in those aspects of their knowledge that will help us to make our shift from limited to full consciousness as easy as possible. Many of these carriers of the esoteric flame of inner knowledge have come into this Earth plane to learn about the nature of Earth's humanity and to participate in this time of ascension. It is to these individuals that this chapter is especially addressed.

For we know that your immense struggle to understand your wonderful body of knowledge has been a challenge. In fact, at times it has been quite an enormous struggle. We can only applaud your efforts and your noble commitment to lend us assistance at this time of need. It is difficult to do those things that you now feel you must accomplish. For many of those around you may still feel the need to maintain the silence that has served your groups and their members in the near and distant past.

However, you should realize that the time has come for this knowledge to be given openly and to be used. Now is a period when the shift in consciousness has become a great river of Spirit that is swiftly flowing towards its final resolution.

Given this situation, it is marvelous to see that many of the

Guardian groups have been able to embrace these new realities. As they do so, they reflect the huge shift in consciousness as well as the new message being given by the Spiritual Hierarchy. This message has embraced our cause and allowed us finally to begin to heal the wounds of spirit that have been inflicted upon us all by our present planetary civilization. It is indeed a most awesome event to bear witness to such a great series of changes.

Let us all take this time to congratulate the Spiritual Hierarchy and the Earth's Ascended Masters for the great task that they have undertaken and are on the verge of completing so successfully. As they accomplish this work, they allow us finally to become a united spiritual family once again — one humanity dedicated to fulfilling its immense spiritual destiny. This destiny will now be accomplished because of the addition of this wonderful group of Guardians who have achieved their task of holding on to the great flame of inner knowledge.

The inner knowledge explained

The inner knowledge has taken many, many forms and it would behoove us to explore it and learn what constitutes it. As we do so, we will show how the many aspects of scientific knowledge that we are only now discovering have a precedent in this vast field of esoteric data.

So let us set foot on this path of discovery. It is a road that has many smaller trails leading into it. Although all of these trails may at first seem fragmented from the main highway, all are nonetheless part of a great assembly of esoteric knowledge.

One of the first fields of knowledge that was given to the Guardian groups was the true nature of the relationship between the subtle energy systems of the body and the body itself. This knowledge in many ways mirrors the concepts of the meridian systems of traditional Chinese and Indian Ayurvedic medicine. However, it goes farther by stating that the source centers for the chakras lie in the back of the body and that the colors traditionally associated with each chakra are rarely in evidence. What is seen is a series of colors around each chakra that indicate the health and the frequency of each chakra in the body.

When viewed as a whole, this series of evaluations can be used to determine the nature of a person's health and how to effect a possible cure. This aspect of esoteric knowledge has been given out in fragments, as the whole concept of healing the body through natural methods has been a controversial subject since the beginning of the 20th century.

In addition, this important knowledge was divided into a number of systems that could aid the body in its healing. These included the use of color, sound, crystals, laying on of hands, and special herbal potions to effect a successful cure. Some of the methods and their respective devices have survived in a quite closely guarded fashion into the modern age.

Their usage has been given out only in a sporadic fashion and at times has been channeled to those special individuals whom the Masters felt could make this great knowledge more public. For the time has now come to use this knowledge and allow those who have enabled it to survive to come forward. There is much that is to be learned, and it is the purpose of this end time that it now be taught and be given out publicly.

Therefore, let us ask that those who have this knowledge establish, with our support, the ways and the means to divulge this vital information. In fact, if possible, let this information be on the curriculum of the Life/Light centers. It is our firm hope that this necessary series of arrangements can be accomplished before the end of this particular year.

Another of the esoteric forms of knowledge given to Guardian groups involves the true nature of matter and its relationship to light. This important series of subjects, which relates to the whole foundation of modern physics, was first given to humanity in very ancient times and was then lost. In the Middle Ages, the knowledge was distorted by what is now called alchemy and passed on correctly to only a few honored initiates.

By the beginning of the 19th century, the advent of modern science had caused many of the initiates to ask permission to form small groups of properly trained and motivated individuals. It was their purpose to bring the keeping of this esoteric knowledge into a more modern framework. Such groups were the forerunners of many of the present Guardian groups who now control a large part of this great body of knowledge.

By the middle of the 20th century, numerous individuals started to receive channeled information from the Ascended Masters
about the true nature of this material. In many ways, this subject
mirrors and surpasses the knowledge being gleaned by scientists
from their data collection and experiments on the relationship of
matter to energy and especially to light.

Light, vortexes, dimensions and changes in a particle's frequency and spin are a key element of this knowledge. Moreover, it
teaches us that life itself is essential to the overall equation. By
studying these subjects, we begin to see that Spirit can be a part of
science and that science is really a means to measure and quantify
Spirit.

In this fashion, humanity learns of the vast powers of Creation
and how Creation has a special place within it for all forms of sentient being. This knowledge also teaches us about the true nature
of karma and the laws of karmic interaction — topics that are
extremely important to us. We are presently growing into a new
form of higher and ascended consciousness. This consciousness
needs to be acknowledged by us and therefore we need to understand its many implications.

One of the most basic aspects of this tremendous weave of esoteric information involves the very essence of what life really is and
how it is maintained. We have to recognize that life and its spiritual essence are intertwined and that life comes from the great light
of Creation.

The source of this light is the central and eternally located higher dimensions of creative energy or what we call the Angels and
Archangels. These agents of change operate according to a series
of special elements, the most important of which is time and the
second most important of which is light.

Time can be visualized in many, many different ways. Our present third-dimensional concept is the most primitive and most distorted version. Time determines life, for it regulates the reactions
that produce life.

Light, in turn, aids time by creating the dimensional vortices
that make it possible for time to exist in its multitudinous forms.
These interactions create the different levels of Creation and give

each level its degree of uniqueness. So, as we can see, time has a very important part to play in the process of Creation.

What also needs to be acknowledged is that time has a different reality in each set of dimensions. Hence, it is an element of great change and also the underpinning of the basic order of physical reality. Time is, therefore, a great Lord of Creation. It establishes the nature of the vortex that creates all matter and determines how matter interacts with itself to create the dimensional limits of any particular aspect of Creation.

One major group that has given a glimpse into the true face of time is the classical Mayan civilization that existed in its full glory in the first millennium after Christ. This civilization has left behind a great and wondrous legacy. However, its concepts of time have yet to be fully understood by our present civilization.

Many of the ancient concepts uniquely mirrored by the Maya are explained in the esoteric knowledge that has long been secretly kept in India, China, and in other parts of the Americas. It is now time for these explanations to be appended to the great Mayan calendar so that a true appreciation of Galactic Time can be given to this now quickly evolving planet.

We have to perceive time as a key ingredient in this whole process of alteration and ascension of our consciousness. For as we approach the spiritual energies of Creation and the meaning of light in its most comprehensive form, we enter the realms of a new reality. This new reality is dominated by accepting a new concept of what really constitutes Time. Time is how light and life come together. It is the great experiential regulator of physical reality.

As time is recognised as the critical aspect of our newly emerging consciousness, we will begin to see it as an all-important element in the Creation. For all things happen according to the great time-line of Creation. It is this time-line that regulates the distribution of creative 'light' in its various aspects throughout Creation and allows us to 'know' when all things are about to happen. Time therefore has an important role to play in maintaining Creation.

This role is also influenced by the spread of the great creative 'light'. It is this 'light' that ultimately determines the nature of each creative dimension . As it does so, it establishes the relationships between life and time. This process determines the true nature of dimensional intelligence and allows for the giving of sentiency to physical beings such as ourselves.

When we are once again returned to our fullest levels of sentiency, we shall begin to understand the importance of time and light and the interrelationship of both elements with life. This reality lies at the basis of all esoteric knowledge. As we begin to get a more complete understanding of life, we shall be able to view all of science in a new way.

This vast paradigm shift is now under way. As it continues, it will allow us to gain a better understanding of how all of Creation is bound together. It is a most marvelous mechanism and its full disclosure will allow humanity to take its place as one of the major benefactors of the energies of Creation in this particular dimension. As we head toward this great destiny, we should have a better perception of what constitutes our reality.

Life is part of a vast system of interrelated mechanisms that together serve as creator and regulator of each dimension. Spiritual energy and its many vibrational forms create the limits and the effects that characterize every dimension.

Each dimension, in turn, has a specific relationship to all other dimensions. The various fluxes that act as dimensional 'walls' function in much the same way as a plant's cellular walls use osmosis to transmit nutrients and excrement from one cell to another — except, instead of nutrients and excrement, the dimensional fluxes move spiritual energy from one dimension to another. The basic difference lies in the role of time. For time is an element that can use this flux region to transmute space and alter the location of any reality that exists in the same dimension as itself.

Light, especially the interdimensional spiritual form, contains within it the possibilities for life. To manifest these possibilities, light must be transformed by time. For time has the capability to determine the nature of life and from it extract magnetism and gravity. It is these two elements that set the boundaries for light to transform itself into the many different forms of life.

When the proper boundaries have been extracted, light can then re-establish itself within a new special set of realities and become life or spirit. This spirit when acted upon once again by time can, as we have stated, create all the different forms of life that exist in this universe.

It is this magic that creates life that the Guardian groups have so deeply resisted divulging to humanity. For they believed that with its full disclosure humans in their limited consciousness would badly distort it and play havoc with Creation. It is now appropriate during this end time to discard this belief and begin to set the stage for a full disclosure. The time has come for all things to be known and for all who hold this knowledge to reveal it to a public that is now preparing for full consciousness.

Summary

Let us therefore conclude this brief chapter by continuing to give our thanks to those Guardian groups that have kept these great esoteric traditions alive. It is my hope and desire that they will see the light and begin the process of disclosing the great amount of knowledge that they possess. By so doing, they will allow us to take back the heritage that this present civilization has tried so hard to prevent us from knowing.

This knowledge is the miraculous gift that was given to us by the Ascended Masters and has been protected by the many Guardian groups that still exist around this planet. We must honor those groups and the great suffering and work that it has taken to keep this knowledge in a usable form.

We therefore ask them to come forward and to pass this precious flame of inner knowledge on to us. We are ready for this great gift and we need this information to aid our journey to higher consciousness. So, let them consider within themselves and realise that now the time is indeed right for a full disclosure of this wonderful data. A world about to ascend is most ready to listen to and be trained by these glorious keepers of the flame of inner knowledge.

THREE

Forming a Planetary Advocate Group

If we are going to form Planetary Advocate Groups, we have to understand the primary purpose of such a group. A Planetary Advocate Group's major purpose is to demonstrate a unique way of applying human spiritual and organizational energy to the major problems now facing our planet and our solar system.

In accomplishing this feat, these groups will help to set the stage for a new galactic civilization. Moreover, they will also give this planet vital human resources for mutual support and counseling that will help to ease the transition from our present society to the one envisioned by the Spiritual Hierarchy. We are part of a divine destiny to change our planet, our solar system and our galaxy into the great beacon of spiritual light that it is ultimately to become.

Problems facing PAGs

Among the major problems that we will face are those conditions associated with the raising of human and planetary consciousness; the ending of human individual, racial and national karmas; and the present breakdown of the traditional forms of human governance. One of the first things I was told by the Galactic Federation is that there are a number of major factors for a positive consideration when looking at these difficult situations currently facing planet Earth.

These major factors include: the increase in the involvement of our Spiritual Hierarchy in Earth human destiny, the position of planet Earth as a major showcase planet for this galaxy, and the five stages of the crystalline Earth that will result in a new series of Earth grids and a new 13-node and 20-faceted planet. We have to remember that this is a transitional period in human history. In such a period, many of the processes of change (resolutions of national, regional and global karmas) may come across as a seemingly vast set of problems.

Our chief concern should be with the spreading of information about this planetary transition in consciousness and the great need to give support to our human family. For as modern biology has proven, we are all interrelated. We breathe the same air. We even use each other's biological materials to make our cells, to form our RNA/DNA, and to energize our bodies. We are all deeply inter-connected and to survive we truly need each other's support on mental, emotional, spiritual and physical levels.

That is why our human morality teaches us about the sanctity of life, the abominable horror of murder, and the unacceptability of practicing wanton cruelties towards each other. We must realize that we are messengers of love and of light.

To be so first requires that we understand the importance of mutual support and the accompanying principles of personal sov-ereignty. These principles and purposes are founded on an inner self-esteem as well as a mutual recognition of each other's gifts, abilities and inner soul purposes. To accomplish this noble series of objectives, we first have to understand ourselves thoroughly on all levels (physically, emotionally and spiritually) and also be aware in great detail of the vast changes now going on around us.

The importance of personal sovereignty

Personal sovereignty and self-esteem work hand in hand to produce the elements needed to create an empowered inner or uncondi-tional love in each of us. We should remember that we are born with a great reservoir of this unconditional love and with an unlim-ited belief in our abilities. Each of us has the potential to contribute those pieces of the puzzle needed to solve all the problems that we may encounter. We are each a part of a vast mosaic of sentient life that surrounds and protects our planet and our solar system.

What usually occurs is that this reservoir of unconditional love and unlimited belief is dried up by the continuous drought of low-ered self-esteem created by our childhood. Moreover, lack of belief in ourselves is in itself a by-product of a society that teaches the art of limitation.

From the beginnings of life on this planet until our cycle here is completed we are presently inundated with the mutual concepts of lack and of limitation. These concepts are constantly being reinforced in us by the competitive nature of human civilization and by the disuniting economic structures that presently engulf human society. These various factors combine to limit even the most successful of humans into realities that are far less than they could otherwise achieve.

We are now in an age of relearning how to achieve our own empowerment and we are beginning to apply it to our lives and our environment. We must utilize these self-empowering abilities as well as respond to the accompanying need give ourselves and others the support required to accomplish our and their objectives and our mutual soul purposes.

So one of our key activities is to come together and learn how to 'just do it'. We must learn the power of commitment and how it can alter the fate not only of nations or planets, but also — and especially — of our own lives. Please learn to be empowered and realise the importance of being able to 'just do it'.

How to get started

Among all the factors that help the formation of any group is a very major, although simple, one. All light workers have to understand that you need a core group of fellow light workers to start a Planetary Advocate Group. This core group of like-minded and like-hearted others can serve as the foundation for a successful PAG because it will contain the elements needed for its success.

Once you have decided to create the group, let a core group form around you. When the group has collected, then it can decide its purpose by putting together a list of what you and your cohorts want initially to accomplish and then another based on your deeper, longer-range goals. When you make these lists, be creative in your desires. Make an inventory of everyone's talents and abilities and then use this resource as the means to put together your list of goals and purposes.

Once you have made these series of lists and set up a general charter for operating your group (an organisational directive — more about this process in Chapters 4 and 5), you should begin to work on one of the goals you have listed. Also be sure to communicate with us about your existence (see information in back of this book about joining *VictoryNet* and getting on our mailing list) so that we can put you in contact with other like-minded local groups and with our liaison in your particular area. In this way, we (*Victory-Net* and my cohorts in Berkeley, California) can act as a clearing-house for solving problems and also as a source of information for others on how you have solved some of the problems that might vitally impact another Planetary Advocate Group's growth.

Remember, we are in this situation together and we need to learn to support each other and also to give praise for actions that help us achieve our goals.

One of the major ways to form a group is to use a previously existing core group — a meditation group, an actual Guardian group or a new group of light workers who have come together to share their abilities as well as their growing consciousness. In some cases such a group may be a combination of all of the above.

A PAG's main purpose

A Planetary Advocate Group's main purpose is to use its growing consciousness. The increased abilities of the group to gather and recognize intuitive knowledge can be used to understand the many concepts and various amounts of information surrounding the shift from limited to full consciousness that will be given to us. Each group will also have to understand its own basic underpinnings as well as the proper applications of fluid management.

In addition, each group will have to possess an innate broad scope of abilities that will allow them to prepare for and inform others of the new and constantly rising waves, or stages, of human and planetary consciousness. To do this important work, it will be necessary for these groups to have a series of trainings. These train-ings will allow their members to better understand and better pre-pare themselves and others for the even more rapid coming changes in human consciousness.

Each PAG must also spread the vital information that will be given to them about the Galactic Federation's mass landings scenar-ios. Furthermore, they will have to maintain a comprehensive worldwide directory of all Life/Light centers and Planetary Advo-cate Groups, as well as of those in their immediate region.

A PAG's primary purpose will be to act as a beacon for any person in their area who is going though difficulties — physically and/or emotionally — that are the by-products of rapid growth in consciousness. To accomplish this vital function, PAGs will need to have the necessary training (mentioned above) that will be provided by the Life/Light centers.

Each Planetary Advocate Group should be able to network with all other groups in order to provide the support required to set up the training of counselors and also to help others to understand the whole process of change that is now moving our Earth human society from a planetary culture to a galactic one. We have to reach a deep realization that we all are part of a huge growing chain of consciousness. To be effective, the links of this chain must constantly be reaffirmed and dynamically utilized.

The vital need to network information

To carry out this function effectively, each member of the group first has to adopt and then understand the intentions and the underlying purposes of a Planetary Advocate Group. Thus, each of us has to see how these concepts that are the foundation for the dynamics of a Planetary Advocate Group can be related to the current purposes of our own meditation and/or Guardian group.

In considering this addition to their own purposes, each group will have to evaluate what they have accomplished by means of their own particular dynamics and use this evaluation as a basis to go over the materials and information on PAGs given to them.

It is important to remember that each group will have a unique part of the puzzle to master and it is its responsibility to convey this purpose (which may shift depending on conditions) to each member and to other groups. The key is to learn how to integrate this purpose with new information and with new members. We have to be reminded at all times that we are dealing with a very dynamic and rapidly changing reality.

In this manner, PAGs can successfully integrate any new information given to them into their own internal group dynamics. This may be as little as a need to better understand the process of fluid management and/or how to put it into practice in the very dynamic environment of a group. Above all, we must learn that we are dealing with a very unique and very 'fluid' situation. This great fluidity is both our greatest strength and our greatest challenge.

By so doing, each meditation or Guardian group can develop the procedures needed to successfully introduce the new dynamic energy associated with fluid management into their respective group. Furthermore, this new energy and the new information that surrounds it will allow any group to be easily transformed and will also allow the group's energy to create its own unique dynamic.

Group dynamics and networking

By using the process of fluid management, each group will have a means to develop the group's energies more easily and to allow themselves to successfully link up with other groups and individuals in their community with whom often they have not previously been involved. In effect, PAGs and their members begin to catalyze their community as well as each other with the new energies that we are now receiving from our planet and especially from its Spiritual Hierarchy.

Basically, most Guardian groups and meditation groups have up till now worked inwardly (deeply involved in the vast and complicated processes of the 'inner planes'). This particular process stems from the deeply held belief that what they are doing is being accomplished on other spiritual planes, which requires an individual spiritual effort.

As a matter of fact, many of the Guardian groups have a deep-seated feeling of exclusivity — a deep need to refrain from contacting each other. This old scenario is based on the fact that many such groups consider their work to require a special body of knowledge that those persons inside the group most readily represent.

The new scenario that we wish to encourage is that we see each other as a necessary part of a greater whole — a mosaic of spiritually minded groups that can work in concert to anchor the light and to stabilize the planet and its Earth human populations. We have a deep need to end secret or esoteric limits to intergroup dynamics.

We want to encourage Planetary Advocate Groups to interlink with one another — to meet with one another, meditate together, work on projects side by side, build a deep relationship with one another.

As they do so, they will begin to see that their way of accomplishing objectives is actually very similar, even though their specific goals may be very different, just as each individual has his or her own concept of reality and spiritual growth. Importantly, the idea of these groups coming together is to enlarge the whole! For when we act as a whole, we can accomplish a most incredible and wondrous magic.

This fact is extremely important and is being encouraged so that each part of this enlarged whole can get evidence of what it is that they are doing and then have the necessary guidance within their own group dynamic to understand these concepts. When PAGs learn how to grow within this newly emerging vitality, they can then move outward.

The key concept is to look at the growing consciousness as if it is in constant movement. One might see it as a constantly outward- and upward-moving spiral. This spiral of group and growing individual consciousness has the ability to move people together, to aid their communications with each other and to provide a means to link up and support their new and very vital activities. It is the magic to which we have just alluded.

The inward-outward spiral effect

What I call the inward-outward spiral is created when the energy of spirit or higher consciousness comes into an individual and develops in its own unique way, while at the same time another energy — a group consciousness or communication energy — which I call the outward spiritual energy, spirals outward.

This energy that spirals outward is represented by the way a person takes what he or she has spiritually received and transmits it to others (on this and other dimensions) and then from this information creates a message that can be presented to others.

This interaction is the communication and liaison process that occurs in these groups. It is occurring right now on a different level with people who are in meditation and Guardian groups. What we are asking is that they look to what they are doing within their specific meditation or Guardian groups and begin communicating that to others. We are asking them to spread their message which is based upon their inner and/or esoteric knowledge.

Now, to further emphasize the whole procedure, what we are doing is first of all to have these groups come together and participate in working on various exercises in fluid management, so that they can gain expertise in how it operates, because it is a new concept. They have to learn to trust each other's intuition and their inner purposes.

Moreover, it is learning how to flow with the inner energies and how these inner energies link with one another, and you see how every person, as they link, has a general gift or ability; and as they understand what their gift or ability is they can then — just like fingers acting in coordination — work more effectively together. The time has come to link together on a global basis in order to help create the new reality.

I would also like to have people meet with Planetary Advocate Groups that are already in operation. My hope is that we will have these groups in operation before the end of this summer and that other groups as they are now forming around the country and the world can see how these groups operate by visiting them and watching them work.

I want to be able to have audio and video tapes and various other media resources such as a satellite television link-up available by the late Fall. We want the Planetary Advocate Groups to be able to utilize them through the use of various worldwide Life/Light centers.

Individuals who are interested can go to the centers and see in detail how PAGs operate and how they achieve their successes. Everyone can then utilize their regional PAGs and Life/Light centers in their own unique way to develop their consciousness and to learn more about themselves and the planet. This is the key to the whole process.

Learning to understand the process

Now, once you begin forming a Planetary Advocate Group, you might say, well what is the guardian process exactly? The first thing that has to be understood is the Earth guardianship role of human society and how it relates to human spirituality.

If you have been exposed to any of my other materials, you will have understood that there is a guardian triangle: the first leg of the triangle represents the Spiritual Hierarchy (SH), the second leg the cetaceans (CET) and the third Earth humans (EH). This is the guardianship triangle.

We are all part of this eternal process, and we have to understand our stewardship of the planet and our stewardship of this entire Milky Way Galaxy. We have to come to a deep understanding that this immense stewardship is based upon our innate spirituality. And we have to recognize that our spirituality is the key to how this world reality operates, because it controls the physical realms.

The problem we often have is that we look at the physical as being the key when we try to translate the spiritual into the physical. In so doing, we forget the energy of the spiritual and how it relates to our being physical. This link point, this changeover point, is what we are now mastering. We have to understand this guardianship process as part of the entire reality shift to make us fully conscious.

The guardian process is also what sets PAGs apart from the spiritual groups that existed beforehand. We now realize the important contribution that the indigenous inhabitants or traditional human guardians of our planet can make to us. Namely, they have the ability to help us understand both the various, quite complex ceremonies and rituals and the lifestyle needed for a successful guardianship.

The dynamics of guardianship

We have to learn about the importance of ritual and the necessary requirements to perform successful and meaningful ceremony. To those of us caught up in a Western lifestyle which emphasizes the vulnerability of the individual and the weakness of groups, it is indeed difficult to view all things as a sacred vessel encased in a profound otherworldly dynamic.

Yet it is important for us to conceive of the notion that full consciousness leads towards a whole new view of reality. It is this new paradigm of ritual and ceremony that we shall now have to embrace.

Summary

To summarize, we are now in a period that requires a new type of organization. This new organization which I am calling a Planetary Advocate Group has the ability to combine aspects of light work that have not until now been group-directed. This ability comes from the group's special dynamic which is created by 'fluid management' and by an increasing human and planetary consciousness.

Our need is to interlink these now forming organizations and to take advantage of the new communication tools currently in use. We also need to fully utilize the even newer state-of-the-art technologies that will be offered to us — more on these developments when we discuss Life/Light centers.

FOUR

Planetary Advocate Group Networking

We shall now consider how Planetary Advocate Groups communicate with each other and, more importantly, give a brief overview of how PAGs can relate to their respective communities. Let us begin by addressing the ways in which such groups can most effectively interact with their own communities.

PAGs and Guardian groups

In every community there will be a number of very important and long-standing Guardian and/or meditation groups that for many years or even decades have held a weekly meeting for meditation and/or discussion of esoteric knowledge. Many of these groups have previously kept themselves very aloof.

They have behaved in this particular manner because each group considered its work to be only for those who were committed to its philosophy and who were prepared to do group meditation in a way that their leaders felt was appropriate for their assigned task.

Such groups should be approached carefully since they are very sensitive to their particular spiritual responsibilities. However, it is necessary to inform them of the changes that are now occurring on the planet and the need to come together to create the new galactic civilization.

In many cases where I have addressed these types of organizations, it has been necessary to let them intuitively feel the truth of the information we are presenting. The key is to inform each group sincerely of the data that now exists about the physical and spiritual changes happening to every individual on the planet.

You should ask them to read the available material about planetary and personal ascension and discuss it among themselves. If they are still interested after their group discussions, ask them to attend a meeting of your Planetary Advocate Group. During this meeting ask the Guardian and/or meditation group if they will consider the possibility of transforming their group into a PAG. Inform them that such groups have a need to do what is in their joy (purpose) and that it would be a good idea if they could also arrange for a joint meeting with any other long-standing Guardian groups who profess to have a similar purpose.

The key point is to constantly be of service to them and help these Guardian and/or meditation groups understand that we are entering a new reality in which creation and a sharing of knowledge is vital. It is important that our local spiritual community understand the essential need to begin to cooperate and to drop their desire to train every potential member slowly in their esoteric knowledge.

They should be impressed with the fact that our global community is quickening to prepare for the coming great shift in human and planetary consciousness. This realization should lead to a sharing of knowledge in the community between the new PAGs and the groups based on much older realities. It is necessary to comprehend that each generation of groups and individuals has kept a great and ancient heritage alive.

This spiritual heritage has now emerged to touch everyone in ways that until this decade were scarcely possible. The beauty of this ending time for our present civilization is that this series of barely connected spiritual groups has managed to set the stage for a new galactic civilization. These various groups, associations and institutions have aided us and they should be honored. They must also be given the essential information they require so that their charters and procedures can be suitably amended. By so doing, each group will be acknowledging the rising movement in consciousness and will be giving validity to what we are all now in the process of accomplishing.

We all have to remember that what we are doing is part of a process of a great change in consciousness. A major aspect of this movement is learning to acknowledge each other. We are here only to do the work of Spirit. This work requires that we now begin to communicate with each other. The entire spiritual community in any area should be informed of what we are doing and be given the opportunity to become a part of this great change in our conscious reality.

Furthermore, we must take into account that each member and each group of this older spiritual community has knowledge and insights that can be of substantial help to us in creating the foundation for our galactic society. We must realize that as the ever-expanding level of consciousness moves out into the community it greatly affects these Guardian and/or meditation groups. They are looking for an answer to what is happening. It is our responsibility to provide it to them and then let them intuitively decide upon its truth.

The critical need for 'spiritual networking'

This coming together of the older and the newer spiritual groups will permit the light workers to start to connect their groups together and begin a process of better understanding those purposes and creative solutions that each group and each individual has to offer to the 'big picture'.

This operation of searching for an inner purpose can lead to the next major step in bringing our worldwide spiritual communities together as quickly as possible. Remember, the energy of Spirit is now working to cause this change in consciousness to happen at a truly unbelievable rate! I call this aspect of change the power of 'spiritual networking'. Let us now look at some of its many principles.

As just mentioned, we are to connect and build our groups by applying the principles of 'spiritual networking'. This term simply means *using the power of group meditation and the useful energies from the new links that we have formed with each other to help give birth to positive change in our spiritual community*. This is a very important point.

In the past, there has been a great deal of fragmentation and a feeling among many groups that they were either competing with one another or that no one else had as much 'correct information' about a certain subject as they did. This belief has led to a great deal of distrust or loss of support in the spiritual community. Another associated problem is a spiritual dissolution or loss of unity from one group to the other.

One of the things I would ask advocate groups to do would be to have what I call special spiritual gatherings for the purpose of allowing a 'spiritual revitalization' to begin to take place in our various communities. These special gatherings should take the form of a meditation along with a discussion with questions and answers that can allow people to come to understand and to 'feel' these new energies of higher consciousness being activated around them.

This type of gathering (a 'bringing together') has the added bonus of allowing various groups to better understand the need to create with one another. Moreover, it stresses the point that their special knowledge is integral to the whole community. The time has come for it to be shared. I can only emphasize the importance of sharing our knowledge and our experiences. This information is the life blood of our global movement.

As they feel the energies, each person will sense the positive change that the energies can create in any person around them. They themselves, as a result of these interactions, will also begin to change in ways that they have yet to fully understand. As they begin to transform, this alteration in consciousness and in body will become more evident to them.

These after-effects will further amplify the outcome that we are looking for. Namely, all the individuals and groups involved will feel a deep need to begin to interact more with other similar spiritual groups and to become more curious about what is happening to them. This will also make the task of forming additional Planetary Advocate Groups and linking them together a much easier operation.

It is very important to realize that we are now in a period of rapid change. This time is one in which the miraculous becomes possible and the remarkable a commonplace event.

This is the key point. We are indeed in a period of rapid change. This transformation/ascension process is one that has to be completed before the end of the year 1996 — little more than a year away at the time of writing. Hence, there can only be an increased amount of energy that favors our success in forming, expanding and linking together our PAGs. It is essential that we understand the vast amount of energy that is being expended daily by the Spiritual Hierarchy and the Galactic Federation on our behalf. This energy completely assures us that as we approach the formation of any PAG with an aura of positive and enlightened purpose it will be a successful endeavor. However, we have to remember that all such activities should most assuredly be approached with a truly positive attitude and a deep, purposeful sense of joy.

The 'activation process'

As more and more of our spiritual community has a chance to experience the power of the newly evolving consciousness, they will go through what I have been calling an 'activation'. This activation allows the individual a brief glimpse of his or her role and purpose in the coming spiritual transformation.

This glimpse also allows for the transformation of various groups, because it deeply affects each group member in a most profound way. Each person begins to sense that their changes are part of a greater human and planetary transformation. A new collection of spiritual realities begins to set in. Humans of such a high level of spirituality are able to embrace these newly forming realities.

Once we have experienced this glimpse of spiritual reality, it becomes almost impossible for us ever to be the same again. One of the first things that occurs is that our physical, emotional, mental and spiritual changes become vastly accelerated.

As this process of transformation increases, we also develop a great need to share this experience and to learn the meaning of the changes now happening around us. This need adds to our anxiety to become part of this overall vast shift in consciousness. Hence, the process of activation is one of the major tools that the Spiritual Hierarchy has given us.

We should realize that our groups are meant to come together in joy for the purpose of allowing all of us to be supported in our divine mission. This mission is one that we are now discovering together.

It is one of our greatest strengths. We must always remember that we are all great spiritual beings going though a limited consciousness experience. Our limited set of consciousness has caused us to experience a severe bout of temporary collective amnesia.

This amnesia often takes hold of us and can, at times, throw us off course. Because of this we have to learn to expect what occasionally will appear as a giant rock that bars our path. However, we need to be able to draw on the mutual support that our PAG should give us and thereby overcome all difficulties.

We are the vestige of a very gregarious sentient species that has come to this planet to establish a new creative civilization at this time. Hence, there is a constant need to understand the limitations imposed by our present civilization. Remember — we put them there. It is timely now to release them.

It is time to support ourselves and to feel the joy that such a support can create. We have within us the ability literally to move spiritual mountains and to change the course of our destiny. Let us now release our own self-imposed limitations and belief systems.

This present period of our reality is to be the final one in which such possibilities for failure can exist. Let us dedicate this time to accomplishing our lofty spiritual goals, realizing that we have the abilities of Angels — because we *are* Angels.

We are the carriers of a great destiny. We are part of a great cosmic transformation which will create a light that will combine with darkness to form the even greater spiritual light of this sixth creation.

We are here to accomplish the great ascension of this planet, of this solar system, and of this galaxy — indeed, of all Creation. This wondrous task is one that is thoughtfully given by the great Archangels of Creation. This particular group of humanity has come to accomplish a most miraculous assignment.

This assignment means that we must establish our groups and a worldwide network that allows us to create successfully with one another. We have to understand that our responsibilities are very great and that we have been amply provided with the abilities to accomplish them. Therefore, we only need to look upon ourselves as a vast resource truly capable of fulfilling our important cosmic destiny.

The need to influence society and help the new light workers

Now, let us go to another step. This step involves linking groups of light workers together to influence society's decisions. Once we have begun the process of creating our groups and of bringing in the older Guardian groups, we need to make a space for those new light workers who are just now beginning their own spiritual awakening.

One of the really good things about this movement is that it involves the older and more traditional realities of consciousness transformation as well as the vastly newer forms. We are here to be conduits for a new reality. As such, we have a deep responsibility to help and assist those individuals who are completely new to this whole process of spiritual ascension.

These vast groups of individuals are people who have yet to have an interest or inclination to be part of this spiritual movement. We need to realize that they are the majority of persons who will become involved with the processes about which we are now becoming knowledgeable. Therefore, it behooves us to see them as a group with whom we may share our knowledge and, most importantly, our assistance.

And we should be prepared to give it. These individuals, when they understand the nature of the changes, will become the core groups for already created and new Planetary Advocate Groups to be established on this planet in the coming year. This fact means that we have to utilize a great deal of networking and modern technology to get our message across to them in a very rapid manner.

As previously stated, the way to do this is through establishing a system of 'spiritual networking'. This system of high technology networks is the second part of the many, many aspects of 'spiritual revitalization'.

It is necessary to understand that right now there are a lot of people on this planet who are just beginning to have an awareness of spiritual consciousness. As they develop, they begin to search for reasons why they are so interested in spiritual matters.

One of the first expressions of this new awareness is an interest in religion. However, this interest soon spills over the rigid boundaries of organized religion and leads these seekers on a truly spiritual quest. This fact is the real reason why books on Angels, Near Death Experiences (NDE) and the unexplained mysteries of life have recently come to the forefront of the world's bestseller lists.

As they continue onward, these seekers become enthralled with the concept of physical and spiritual ascension as well as with the entire UFO phenomenon. These seekers of a new reality are also

In La Kech (a Mayan greeting which means "I am another yourself").

s of physical, emotional and spiritual
now experiencing. They are our broth-
being helped.

ve each PAG set aside time for them.
ated into the true realities that are tak-

is our responsibility to set up numer-
eventually a television training sys-
rapid education. We are working with
the one that up till now has allowed
onscious'.

get to support each other in our own
d also that we will have to take on the
orting those who have yet to be a part
spiritual groups and associations. We
nave to realize that our movement is more than just a local one —
it is one that is global in scope.

The resources have been provided

In addition, we have to remember that as a group we have the
resources to complete our vital assignment. During the last few
months of this year, the fiscal and management components for our
projects will begin to appear. These resources will make possible
the successful completion of our duties. As one might say, the best
is yet to come.

This abundance in money and other vital resources has been
made possible through the spiritual manifesting energies that the
Ascended Masters have given this planet. So because the time was
spent to focus on and to utilize these energies, we will be gifted
with the necessary resources.

We should remember that they have been given to us as part of
the grand divine plan to establish a new galactic civilization on our
planet and because we as a people were ready for it and had prepared ourselves for it.

For that reason, many wondrous things are starting to happen
that will aid our ability to complete the Life/Light centers on time.
These centers will serve as the nodes for the communication and

training networks that are required to complete the grand plan.

The grand plan as it now stands

The scheme, at the present time, is to put between 100 and 300 of these centers into operation by the end of next summer (1996). This plan would seem an almost impossible task if it were not for the great deal of creation that is already coming forward on a world-wide basis to complete this tremendously vital project.

It is our hope to have the first prototype center operational on Maui by the end of this Fall and to be able to use it as a model for rapidly establishing prototype centers in Europe, the Americas, Australia, Polynesia, Africa and Asia by early Spring of 1996. It is hoped that the other centers can be established before the end of the Summer of 1996. At least that is the plan as we now speak.

By continuing to move forward as a relatively unified network, we can influence our society's decisions. However, the key point is also to recall that we have a responsibility to aid the indigenous peoples of this planet, the cetaceans who are a part of our guardian triangle, and the planet itself. To accomplish this obligation, I would once again like to emphasize the whole principle of spiritual networking.

We have to realize that as we begin to network among ourselves, we will have the ability to influence society by being a recognized force for higher consciousness and morality. We will have the ability to manifest and to create that will enable us to help change the outlook of society. In this way we will begin to influence our civilization and help it to have a better understanding of the transition that is now going on around us

We must continue to be advocates and liaisons for planet Earth. As I keep saying, I want groups to work together. It is necessary that we impress on the environmental movement the need for unity. This unity must be founded in a joy for life and the new birth of consciousness now flowering on our planet.

As people rapidly become more conscious, they begin to realize the importance of the planet and get an inkling of their future role as planetary guardian. It is this purpose that we must strive to impress on all involved.

This time is one of great transformation and great shifts in the societal realities of what a human culture is supposed to represent. It is our responsibility to set important examples that can help to truly alter the nature of our society.

The ascension process and PAGs

One of the major items that we must discuss is information about ascension and other processes vital to the development of our Planetary Advocate Groups. Therefore, it is necessary that we use our networking facilities to exchange information about this particular process and also about those other developments that are occurring on the planet. It is important that we are informed on what is happening locally as well as globally.

To do this job, we must exchange information, develop group liaisons, and become knowledgeable about those matters in which we are most interested (the key is to learn and to be able to express in joy and be gifted for our efforts). In this way, we can verify our data and develop a means to correct and substantiate it.

As an example, let us look at the ascension process. The ascension process on Earth consists of two mutually dependent segments. The first part is what I call the rebirth of the Crystalline Earth. We must recognize that our planet and we ourselves are in the midst of a mutual rebirth. This reality is a key point in the whole process. We need constantly to remind ourselves that our planet is a living being going through many of the same processes that have affected us ourselves.

The second aspect of the ascension process involves humans changing from being primarily very dense and limited conscious beings into very highly evolved spiritual and physical beings. We should exchange information between one part of the globe and another that helps to impress this fact on ourselves and on society at large. We have to understand these two aspects of ascension and exchange information between us.

An important part of this whole mix is to involve the mass media as much as possible. In this way, we can inform the mass public as to what is happening and allow them to see that there does indeed exist an alternative to their reality.

As we carry out this part of the plan successfully, we will be able to reach many more persons than we otherwise could. For this reason and many others too numerous to mention, I reiterate that we have to use the media to communicate that there is a spiritual and physical connection between human society and planet Earth.

This is a very important part of the whole procedure. Humans have to understand that the divine plan is for the development of a very deep and very credible spiritual interconnection between humans, the cetaceans, the Galactic Federation of space brothers and sisters and, most importantly, the Spiritual Hierarchy which includes the great and loving efforts of our planet's Ascended Masters.

Summary

The concepts we have just discussed can work together. And the best way to put them into operation is by achieving our purpose through helping the mass public to realize and then utilize these important connections — the grand connection that now exists between human society and human consciousness, as well as the physical and spiritual changes that are now taking place.

The mass public as well as the spiritual community will have to understand why we are in existence and learn how the nature of these concepts of reality truly operates.

This is a very major part of the whole procedure. Therefore one of the things I want to emphasize is the importance of establishing connections with influential individuals and groups in society and making them aware of your group's purpose. Now, this is something that may seem high faluting to a lot of people, but it is a part of the whole process.

And that process, very basically, also includes setting up meditation groups, doing meditations and carrying out other essential spiritual activities that give various leaders — either those who are providing resources or those who are in various important parts of the network on this planet — an idea of what is happening at the local level, at the national level, and at the international level. It is a very vital part of the process and is the reason why ongoing networking is one of the major aspects of the advocate group process.

Five

Fluid Management

One of the major techniques used by galactic humans in their organizations is fluid management. It is based upon two important criteria. The first is personal sovereignty, which is simply *the understanding that all humans have a unique knowledge or talent they can contribute to a group's purpose*. Secondly, it is accepted that each individual has the right and privilege to be honored for their uniqueness and allowed to express their abilities freely to others. We shall discuss these elements in greater detail after we have explained another important point.

The Laws and society

In a galactic human society, all individuals are viewed as being under the protection and the process of the *Four Societal Laws*. These laws regulate society and provide for a system that encourages all members of society to express themselves fully and to use their lives to achieve an aspect or soul purpose that can best move themselves and their society into the great light of Creation.

As such, the individual, from the beginning, is immersed in an environment of high self-esteem and self-worth. A constant love and caring is shown to him/her and there is a sense that one's life is valuable and needed for society to achieve its overall purposes. Such an environment provides a mutually supporting outlook that is combined with a great desire to serve the community — but not in any way that is self-depreciating to the individual.

This concept leads to a great schism that aids the growth of the individual and which can be explained in terms of the *Laws*. The first two Laws refer to the individual and his or her primary relationships, while the last two refer to the relation of the community to the individual.

Each galactic human has a sense of commitment to herself or himself as well as a vitally strong link to community service and the responsibilities that such a commitment represents. This deep sense of commitment or caring for oneself and one's fellows leads to an experience of well-being that is expressed by service. Service consists of two vital aspects.

First, there is a need for service that allows us to completely express this inner caring for self and others by contributing our gifts and abilities to society at large. This kind of service leads us to join organizations and to contribute to them with all of our heart and capabilities.

Second, there is a need for effective ritual that allows us to express our soul purpose as the main reason for physicality — namely, planetary guardianship and the many ways in which it is expressed. This is done through special group ritual at various important temple and sacred sites and by a daily schedule of special prayers and ceremonies that the individual carries out at assigned times and places.

It is out of this world that we begin to see how one can develop the tools needed to make a success of any one life and the society to which it belongs. For each society is seen as a society in process, and the process is based on unconditional love, deep caring and group responsibility. Each of these points serves to define the individual and contribute to their sense of being an effective and worthy part of the much greater whole.

And in this way we release the need to be competitive, since all physical needs are provided for by society. However, there is a very strong drive to utilize and to express one's soul purpose. This great need leads to and contributes to the constant dynamic condition of galactic human society.

Daily life and one's soul purpose

Daily life will consist of exploring our capacities and testing them for how they best aid us in our own journey. Each individual is taught about the ways of the petals of life . Each life (petal) is just one aspect of learning the constantly unfolding knowledge of the physical and spiritual Creations. This knowledge is necessary so that one can rejoin the Creator as one part of the greater light that is needed to bring this particular soul essence and Creation to a successful conclusion.

As a result, all aspects of one's life take on a very sacred and very uniquely important reality. This reality is expressed by service. Yet this service is not to be dictated by others, but by the inner rules, or soul purpose, that were agreed to by your spirit council (your Angelic guides and your Higher Self) before this particular incarnation was formally established.

This primary reality leads to the need for personal sovereignty. Each individual is to be treated as an important sacred being that possesses a message (gift) necessary for society to continue to fulfill its obligations to itself and to its vital guardianship of the planet and star system in which it currently resides.

This important set of mutual responsibilities between individual and society establishes the environment within which all organizations operate. It means that any organization must address itself to the need for achieving its objective within the given framework of personal sovereignty. This immediately implies that to be successful an organization must have a well-defined purpose and a means of allowing all its members to express themselves to the group.

Here is where the key point of sovereignty rises to establish a means for success. Each member realizes that every specific situation requires a specific solution. Therefore, every group is wedded to using a creative process of leaving the floor constantly open to suggestions as a means to generate solutions.

Moreover, the group is beyond having a specific hierarchical pecking order. Depending on the requirements of the group, the leadership can be transferred among its members or the group can be enlarged or even transformed (dissolving into something completely different) according to circumstances.

The organization and personal sovereignty

Organizations are viewed by galactic human society as transitory things that exist to achieve a specific purpose. It is this transitory nature that creates the dynamic which drives the organization towards the achieving of its purpose. As purposes are achieved, organizations can either be dissolved or transformed. That is, an organization can be either absorbed into another group or changed in purpose and/or membership. The conditions for this change are determined by the membership of the organization. Here we must remember that each individual is sovereign and the organization is oriented toward achieving a goal in the context of its members' capabilities.

The key at all times is the individual. Purposes are achieved by the most productive use of the individuals' gifts and *not* the coercive ability of a 'management team'. Indeed, management is not a given task of the group except in so far as it applies to its purpose and how the members feel that it can be achieved.

Management is viewed as a test of how self-sovereignty and caring for others can best achieve one's soul purpose and one's need to be a part of society's desire to successfully attain its objectives. Management, in this regard, becomes a task that is granted to those in the group whom the members feel can best use each person's talents and abilities to allow the group to accomplish its agreed-upon purpose or goal quickly and easily.

This concept allows the responsibility to remain open to those who are most capable at a particular time. In this way, a group of galactic humans can fulfill their purpose and easily achieve a successful outcome. The key here is to fulfill the objective, reach the goal, as quickly and as easily as possible.

Now this approach will also allow the group to go outside itself, if it is agreed that another person not presently associated with the group should come in and offer a successful solution to the problem at hand. In effect, the group is unified within itself, yet remains a part of society as a whole.

This reality implies that even though a group may have a previously defined boundary (in terms of purpose and membership), it is inclusive of anyone who can successfully contribute to it or its purpose. Group membership is always seen as being part of society and so all constituents of society are also members of the group.

Organizations have a natural cycle. They may come, go, or be transformed, but each individual remains sovereign and able to contribute effectively to any organization whether or not they are a member. So in society the individual's rights take priority along with the individual's obligation to express himself or herself to the fullest degree. It is for these purposes that galactic human society was established in the first place.

The individual and 'fluid management'

As people begin to understand who they are, they also begin to realize, very importantly, that they have a specific and unique way of looking at things — in other words a talent. These gifts have been given to every human as a part of their soul purpose for being incarnated. This is true whether one is a fully conscious being or one of limited consciousness.

We have to understand that as we grow more conscious our true talents become more evident. One of the difficulties for beings of limited consciousness is that these talents may be in direct contradiction to what we are actually doing to maintain ourselves in our society. Therefore we have to learn to evaluate ourselves and trust what we come up with. As we go through this simple process, we will learn that like the beings in a fully conscious galactic society we have a purpose and a reason for our existence.

Every person has a specific set of talents or abilities — a particular way of doing things creatively. In the Planetary Advocate Groups we can interact in such a way that permits everyone to consider a certain situation and to complete a certain task effectively.

These abilities are ones that we have usually been thwarted in developing effectively or have not been permitted to use as fully as we would like to. We have consequently experienced a feeling of frustration and these gifts may have lost some of the joy often associated with them.

The main reason for PAGs, besides helping to prepare our planet for the new consciousness, is to bring back this inner joy. Use your gifts to achieve your joy (inner desires) and be of service to the ascension of humanity and the planet as well! Use PAGs to learn how to creatively restore your confidence, joy and feelings of well-being. PAGs exist to help you explore your reality and the joy of acknowledging who you really are. They have been created to permit us to function in ways that sanction our sovereignty and also our service to ourselves and to each other, including our planet. Now is the proper time to make use of them and also to be of service to our transforming society.

'Fluid management', as we have stated, is an open organizing technique that will allow any group to manage itself successfully.

It accomplishes this in two principal ways.

First, the group creates itself from what the members (the founders or its core) want it to be. This arises from each member looking at their own gifts and allowing the serendipity of the situation to creatively form the group and its initial purposes. In this way the group maintains a responsive role in relation both to its members and to its environment.

Second, the group constantly re-creates itself. It allows the environment and its own creative approaches to determine the best way to achieve its intent. Thus, group fluidity is the key. This concept is the keystone of the successful usage of fluid management.

Fluid management and the Federation — an example

We are constantly applying ourselves to our environment in ways that allow our talents and the environment to engage in an exchange of joy. What we do is being done to show our joy and talents to the community, especially to that element that we wish to impact. In turn, we receive feedback of two kinds.

The first is the response to the project that we are promulgating in our joy. The second is the new membership and new resources that amplify the success that this joy has produced. Hence, one aspect leads to helping the other to be more easily attained. The result is a system that is environmentally sensitive as well as membership sensitive. Such a unique system also encourages a specific type of leadership requirement.

Leadership has to be situation-sensitive. Group members have to take turns as leaders according to their strengths and the requirements of a given situation. To give you a better idea of how the concept of leadership operates, let us look at the Galactic Federation as a prime example.

Figure Number 1: *Galactic Federation's Liaison Group Command and Control System*, on page 61, is a general organizational chart of the Galactic Federation, and the point to emphasize here is the liaison and communication system. I want to explain this system so that everyone who looks at it will have a better idea of exactly what fluid management is and how it functions.

It is important for all of us to take note of the fact that this chart,

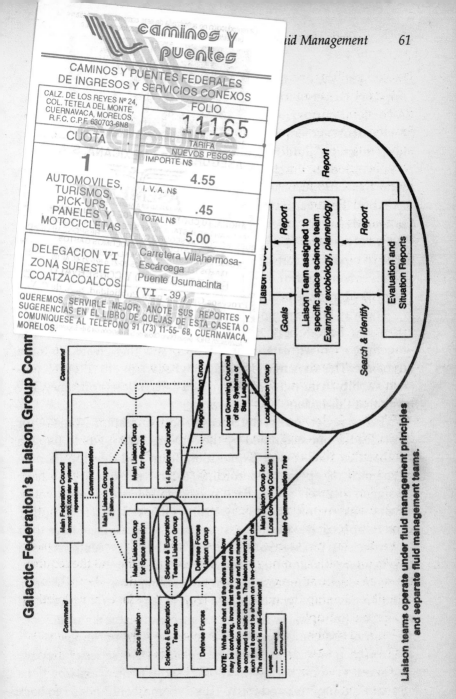

Galactic Federation's Liaison Group Comm...

Liaison teams operate under fluid management principles
and separate fluid management teams.

Figure 1

along with the other organizational chart in this book, is a static imprint of a very fluid — in other words changeable — situation. All Federation operations vary from day to day and this affects how each part or segment of a chart relates to the others. Therefore please keep this rapid fluidity in mind when reviewing this explanation.

Let us look at the chart and its various aspects. Each part represents a specific purpose whose daily process can be changed rapidly. Now, the organization that we are dealing with has its own unique dynamics (operational environment). The liaison group's job involves establishing and maintaining a network for the purpose of rendering constant evaluations. Hence, their main concern involves communications that are centered on these evaluations; it is the holder of the evaluations.

The way fluid dynamics works is that you carry out a task, and then you have a network evaluation. The two processes work together, each with its own specifics, and this creates its own dynamic. This dynamic is based on what we might call each person's ability in the network being used to its fullest proficiency. The way that this is done is as follows:

Let us review one of the Science and Exploration Teams — for instance the one magnified by the drawing. What would happen is that this Science and Exploration Team will develop its own dynamics of operation according to the personnel that have assigned themselves to it. Each person will have their own ability, their own dynamic, and this dynamic will be reflected in the group and its approach to the task assigned. Every person will have their own decision process. So you have your ability (perceptions based upon your gifts) and this gives you your decision process.

Your decision process is then taken by another person with a similar viewpoint who evaluates your results (your decisions and your questions about what is occurring based on the environment's response) and comes back with answers to your questions.

You then provide to the other person another series of processes, and they come back with another series of answers. You get a dynamic going back and forth. This dynamic continues to go back and forth until the group itself performs the task. While the task is being performed, it is being accomplished in complete fluidity which means the concept of reality relating to the task is open. It is fluid — because as it is being realized this process itself can change.

Let me give you another example of the use of this concept. In a very limited way it is used in the present corporate environment. We have the so-called team process or team project, wherein every person down on the assembly line has the right to come up with a decision that could affect the product and how it is put together.

This decision is evaluated by the team leader, who then breaks the decision down and goes up to higher management with a series of suggestions. The team leader, the higher management and the assembly team then all give their feedback about it, and there we have a very limited version of this process of going back and forth.

Now, the aspect that is added to what we see in the corporate scene involves the fact that the Federation chart is an open structure or system. In the case of the network or the Science and Exploration Team, they would use a network group that corresponds — as you can see in the chart — to the particular team.

Thus, every major group has a liaison group that reports back to the main liaison group. The main liaison group will then use the information given to it at higher levels to provide a number of feedback loops and then there is also additional feedback provided in both upward and reverse positions.

Let us take one of these groups and break it down a little bit so you can get a better idea of the whole process. The Science and Exploration Liaison Team breaks down to an S&E team assigned to specific space sciences — for example: exobiology, planetology, etc. — and then that breaks down to a final group, which is an evaluation and situation report group. This last group would consist of one person interacting directly with another person.

These two people are matched because they have similar perspectives on how to undertake a certain process, yet they each have their own unique approach to it. Hence, their approaches are reciprocal, in that they complement each other — making it possible for them to communicate with one another. So, we have goals going down and reports going up. And we create a circle that I call the circle of information and the networking of light and light energies.

What happens in the Galactic Federation is that these groups are occasionally layered upon one another in so far as they are simply providing a larger arena for the answering of questions. These questions involve the situation in the physical universe and a consideration of spiritual reality.

We still have a guardianship working itself out here, and this guardianship means there has to be a spiritual element involved in the decision-making process.

To apply this system to our Planetary Advocate Groups means that we have to keep our responsiveness to our environment at the highest levels of concern and originality. We must be prepared to work out any difficulties and internal blocks that have kept us from our joy.

This requirement means that we have constantly to check ourselves and see that what we are doing comes from our joy. So keep a list of your gifts and compare them with those of your core members and others who are part of the PAG. Also keep a running list of how your members relate to the organizational purpose.

Stay responsive and be prepared to merge or to transform your organization as the environment changes and its potential problems surface. Do not see your participation or present levels of participation in a PAG as a given — be prepared for change and for miracles.

This present time is one that is filled with the wonderful and the miraculous. Learn about yourself, your joys and how to express them. See how you can support others. The results will prove to be quite different than what you may at first expect.

Summary

'Fluid management' encourages group members to discover and explore their abilities and their talents. This is a key point. Every human being is seen as an integral aspect of any organization.

These organizations are what you might call people-oriented organizations as well as spiritually-oriented organizations. This process allows any and all beings, on all levels, both the spiritual and the physical, to work together.

Therefore I look upon fluid management as being a new paradigm or model for the management of people-oriented organizations. This is the key point that has to be emphasized.

Six

Purpose of Planetary Advocate Groups

As we have seen, Planetary Advocate Groups have been established to act as the organization that informs the community about what is happening on this planet — which means that they have a very great and critical mission to perform. This mission involves not only the ascension process of our planet and our human society, but also the need to give support and sustenance to our fellow light workers while they go through their great travails.

These travails are associated with the various processes that arise from the many emotional, mental and physical blocks imposed by our lives in this most limiting civilization. We have to use this unique organization as a kind of shelter from the 'storm' that is rising up around all of us. This 'storm' (the new consciousness) is now being established by the Spiritual Hierarchy to rain down on us like a proverbial flood. Our task is to act as both the prophet and the innkeeper for this new, developing event.

PAGs have an important role to play

Planetary Advocate Groups, as we have noted, will have an important part to play in this great change. However, we should keep sight of our joy and the need to express it in our various communities. For our joy and its various expressions will help to give those around us the support and love they need to go through their changes. A major aspect of this expression will involve learning, using and teaching the dynamics of fluid management.

PAGs are able to demonstrate that such a new way of running an organization can be highly successful. As we work in our environment of purposeful joy, we will have the ability to make a deep impact on our two communities. First, we can greatly aid our fellow light workers and, second, we can show the community at large that there is in existence a 'way station' to a new reality.

Remember that fluid management is a technique that allows all Planetary Advocate Groups to operate as centers for change and also allows your groups to evolve as the conditions around you — your environment — so warrant. It is important to remain constantly fluid and open to suggestions about the organization from the membership. Do those things that will permit you to achieve your objectives, but be sure that these objectives can be attained by the PAG. Be modest in your purposes. Please do what you are capable of and then as your resources quickly grow do the rest. Remember too that we have a divine mission and that as you clear your blocks, miracles can happen.

When you are in a leadership role, be prepared to embody it to the best of your talents and abilities. And be ready to adjust your style when an adjustment is necessary. Do everything in joy and be in a space of total acceptance and growth. Everything that is happening to us is given both as a lesson to be learned and as a task to be performed.

Hence it will provide us with a means to achieve a new view of reality and, most importantly, of ourselves. We are in the midst of applying things that have yet to be carried out on such a grand scale and we have to be cognizant of this fact. So just be in your joy and in your space of total acceptance and growth, so that all of this initial 'sticky stuff' can pass as quickly and as easily as possible.

PAGs as galactic time study groups

Another important step for us is to act as the way-showers to a new and crucial concept of time — galactic time. Galactic time involves changing our reality from the sequential and comparatively limited consciousness of 12:60 time to the galactic and expansive reality of experiential 13:20 time. This new concept of time is based on two important principles. First, the 13-month yearly and 28-day monthly calendar, which incorporates the sacred Mayan *Tzolkin* of 260 kin or days.

Be reminded that each day is composed of a sacred harmony (red, white, blue or yellow), a tone (one of 13 creative tones) and a glyph (one of 20 solar seals). Each kin or day sign allows us to understand the nature of the day and relate it to our birth kin (the kin or day sign when we were born).

This 13-month, 28-day calendar and its relationship to the *Tzolkin* will be studied by the Planetary Advocate Groups. It is essential that PAGs become *galactic time study groups* as well. To accomplish this, an individual from the membership of the PAGs in your local area will be selected as a special liaison to travel to our prototype center and learn how to utilize this vital information and present it to others.

I feel it is very important that this information be explained correctly and that as many people as possible are made knowledgeable about the new calendar. For as we go onto the new calendar in a massive way, the energies of planetary time are being reset and a new reality is being manifested for all of us.

As this new time structure is used around this planet, we begin to experience a new definition of time. Moreover, we begin to set the energies for the fourth- and fifth-dimensional reality shift that is coming with the advent of the new age of light. This new age of light (the *Itza Age* in the Mayan) is now beginning to form all around us. We have to acknowledge it and allow this new energy to bring its light to us. Time is an essential aspect of the creative process in the physical and spiritual universes.

We are going to help this mechanism (galactic time) to achieve its objective. By so doing, we will be allowing this time-energy to lead us to our new era of light. This time also coincides with the setting forth of the fully conscious Crystalline Earth. As our planet and our solar system assume their place of destiny, it behooves us to remove the remaining barriers of limiting 12:60 time and replace it with the expansive energy of 13:20 time. We are doing this because it is now the period of the *Itza Age* and the return (ascension) of full consciousness on this planet and in our solar system.

The importance of the network

The pivotal role of the calendar and the need to learn how to use our galactic time system emphasizes an important point in our discussion, namely the need to see our groups as places for the disbursement of vital information about the changes in consciousness — in other words, the ascension/transformation process. To accomplish this function requires that all of us be linked into our main information center — *VictoryNet* (http://www.victory-net.com/). It is

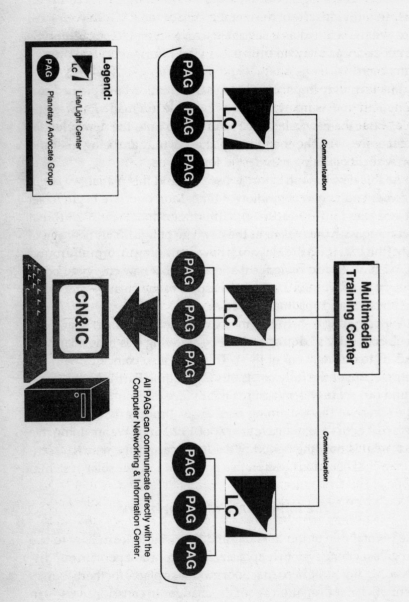

Figure 2

the purpose of this center to act as our electronic newspaper and age of light magazine. It will be used as a bulletin board, a source of important spiritual and changing consciousness information, and a means for us to obtain videos, audio tapes and other materials necessary to carry on the work. In this way, it will allow us to be connected with one another and to keep up to date with what is happening on this planet.

One of the most important things that we can do is to take advantage of these vital links between us and begin to understand how necessary they are to our continued existence. With the use of this system, it becomes possible for potential new members or even potential new Planetary Advocate Groups to have an instant introduction to what we represent.

It will also allow us to schedule conferences on the related subjects of ascension; mental, emotional and physical changes; and the nature of the messages that the Spiritual Hierarchy, Ascended Masters and the Galactic Federation are giving us.

As an added benefit, we can use this system to critique these conferences and consider how the new information is presented. The ability to do this will allow the PAGs and their members to help improve the type of information we give you and the manner in which it is presented.

One of the most vital functions of the Planetary Advocate Groups is to act as support centers for their membership and those in the community who are going though the various changes in reality that are brought on by this new system of rising consciousness. It might be useful for these PAGs to be able to act as the grounding crew for this great change.

One of the most important aspects of this service would be to find and link up with various Guardian groups and/or skilled psychics and healers who have the capability to help 'ground' individuals and allow them to get their changes into a more rational perspective.

This service should aid us and others to understand that this organization is both people-oriented and community-oriented. It has been created to show humanity the way through the great maze presented by the new consciousness. And we wish to show it to them with as much ease as possible. Our purpose is to express joy, cooperation, and above all the fact that the coming era of light can be attained with very little chaos.

A look at how the organization will function

To obtain a better understanding of how our very fluid worldwide 'organization' is going to operate, let us consider the organizational chart (see Figure 2: *Planetary Advocate Groups and Life/Light Centers* on page 68). If you look at the chart, you will see that the key lies in two important nodes — the multimedia training center (MTC) and the computer networking and information center (the CN&IC) or simply *VictoryNet* (a web site for Operation Victory).

Each part of the system connects with the others and all are or will be interactive with one another. The key point to remember is that this is to be a very fluid system that can meet our ever-changing and ever-expanding needs. However, each communication node will also have a major purpose. So let us now review the purposes of these two fundamental nodes of our system.

The first major node is the CN&IC (Computer Networking & Information Center — i.e. *VictoryNet*). This center will be the core for groups to communicate with each other and to obtain information on any special events, spiritual and Federation messages, news of resources available for our needs, and important messages that can be passed from one PAG to another in a distant part of the planet.

The CN&IC also has another major role to play. It is eventually to be set up as an interactive communication system and, as such, it will be able to be used as a forum in which to pass around new ideas and concepts that may help us in creating the worldwide Planetary Advocate Group network. This network is to be used for two purposes.

First, it will provide a directory of the many and varied PAGs that exist in any particular area. This will allow potential new members to contact the PAG that they are interested in.

It will also allow them to see how, if they so desire, to create their own PAG. The CN&IC can help them to discover how this new PAG can link into and receive support and assistance from the already existing PAGs.

Furthermore, any Planetary Advocate Group can use the network to see how it can help other PAGs with their problems. The purpose here is mutual support and we should feel that we can count on each other for assistance. Which brings me to the next node — the Multimedia Training Center and its main component, the Life/Light Centers (LCs).

The Multimedia Training Center (MTC) will be organized in two stages. The first stage is to obtain the moneys to get the global interactive satellite television up and running by the end of this year. When this system has been funded and is on-line, we shall be able to establish a training schedule that allows those at the various centers to interact with the primary trainers at the MTC in Hawaii — which constitutes the second stage mentioned.

The purpose of the Life/Light Centers

We have to establish the Light/Life Centers as quickly as possible and use them primarily as training facilities. In this mode, we would like to take our trainers and move them from center to center so that important concepts about the new consciousness can be made available to all the Planetary Advocate Groups. Moreover, we intend to develop a series of videotapes that will allow us to get the information out to the PAGs as quickly as possible. Now, one may ask, what are these Life/Light Centers? They are to be worldwide in scope and are being set up for two major purposes.

First, they act as places where training can be undertaken and Planetary Advocate Groups can come to them to obtain support for their physical, mental and emotional changes and to learn methods of helping others in their respective communities. Moreover, we intend eventually to use these centers as a resource where the PAGs can come to develop their ideas and share them with other PAGs in their areas.

These 'conferences' will be created on a monthly basis to permit this sharing of ideas, but they will also serve another important end. We have to learn more about one another, become good friends and really know one another. We are all in this consciousness change together and we will have to rely on one another in order to go through it successfully. So it is good to have the opportunity to visit with each other from time to time and these centers will play a social as well as a practical role.

Second, the centers will serve to house state-of-the-art equipment. In this way, it becomes possible to set up training modules for situations that will best lend themselves to this type of environment. The importance of this resource is that it will permit a trainer to concentrate on an individual even in their absence. Hence, a trainer could demonstrate a specific method or technique and thereby allow a trainee or a group to grasp a practical understanding of an important yet obscure procedure.

This capability can also be applied to groups and will greatly enhance our trainer's ability to get a message across easily and quickly to everyone concerned. Hence, these centers will become a focal point for advanced training, for important informational conferences, and for meetings and lectures by and for the area's Planetary Advocate Groups. As the centers are established, each one will quickly develop its own unique character and set of responsibilities.

Each Life/Light Center, in turn, has an important role to play in its own community and for its local Planetary Advocate Groups. These centers are to be places where the general public can be quickly educated in what we are all about.

This vital function will be carried out by means of monthly and possibly weekly gatherings at the Life/Light Center. This will allow the PAGs, the general public and other highly interested and motivated individuals to interact with one another. The hope is that this will encourage participation and also create clear understandings in the community regarding what the PAGs are really about.

Finally, we trust that these Life/Light Centers can be used to establish the means to link those groups which wish to contribute to and/or aid the many PAGs in their area. In many cases, organizations that wish to maintain their identity will be willing to provide aid and assistance. Here, the center can serve as a medium through which initial exchanges can occur and then serve as the liaison between different groups.

In this way we can begin to make a rapid connection with those who are interested in helping us. Moreover, we can use the Life/Light Centers to provide training for the public that can zero in on certain topics even more than the PAGs can do. This capability will allow the centers to assist in getting the message out to the general public. They will also help by providing the computer terminals that will allow anyone to link directly into *VictoryNet* and thereby experience what this vital communication tool is all about

We have to remember that this organization is fully committed to Spirit and to the great consciousness revolution that is now taking place on a global basis. As such, we will have to use our talents to bring all these elements together successfully in a most remarkably short period of time. As we accomplish this immense feat, we will be able greatly to aid the rising and transforming world consciousness. This task is a most monumental one — and we are perfectly capable of achieving it.

Relationship of PAGs to the Spiritual Hierarchy and the Galactic Federation

First of all, Planetary Advocate Groups are the foundation upon which the divine plan for this planet and our human civilization has been laid. Humans have been put on this world as part of the divine plan to create — with this planet's Spiritual Hierarchy —a planet of light, a Crystalline Earth. In effect, Planetary Advocate Groups are the nodes in the great web of consciousness that are being used to lay this divine plan upon our planet. They are important. That is why it is essential that they are formed now.

The next thing to stress is that Planetary Advocate Groups, as I have mentioned previously, will use meditation, rituals, and channeled consultations with the Spiritual Hierarchy to receive guidance on spiritual projects. Basically, these tasks are being performed to heal the planet, to allow you to perceive the nature of the guardianship — to grasp how the PAGs can achieve their full concepts of reality. These particular undertakings are all basically spiritual projects for they live in the natural abundance all around us.

We have to comprehend that to carry out a spiritual intention means that anything can be achieved provided that we learn how to reconnect with our spiritual purpose. To accomplish our spiritual intention, we have to rid ourselves of the mental, emotional and physical blocks that stand in the way of consummating our reality. PAGs are the best places where this new web of consciousness can be explored and where the prophecies of the coming divine intervention can be fully explained.

The Galactic Federation, the divine intervention and us

Now, the divine intervention, as I view it, involves two steps:

First, the Angelic intervention, which is about to happen as part of the ascension process.

Second, the arrival of those fully conscious guardians who are coming here to aid us in achieving our ascension process. They are, of course, the Galactic Federation itself.

Consequently, we now have to explain how the Galactic Federation and the Spiritual Hierarchies interweave and how the whole process is going to take place. This is the key — how Planetary Advocate Groups relate to the Spiritual Hierarchy and the First Contact Team of the Galactic Federation.

Planetary Advocate Groups, as I previously stated, act as the intermediary that prepares human society for membership in the Galactic Federation. Our job is to help humans understand the nature of the guardianship. In accepting the nature of the guardianship, PAGs prepare all of us for membership in the Federation.

By accepting the nature of spiritual light and how light-working interrelates with that concept, they prepare themselves for the process of ascension and transformation. PAGs have to choose the means to spread this knowledge to others.

PAGs will receive information and assistance when the Galactic Federation's First Contact Team's mass landings occur. The First Contact Team is the actual group that will be in charge of preparing for the mass landings and is presently assisting the Spiritual Hierarchy in the changes in consciousness that are happening on this planet.

The Federation's counseling teams will be assisting us through it. And the Planetary Advocate Group's job is to aid the Federation's counselors in providing this service. PAGs accordingly would be the primary human resource for selecting candidates and representatives for the temporary governing councils. Governing councils will consist of cetaceans, selected humans, and selected members of the Spiritual Hierarchy and Ascended Masters. Those humans assigned to the specific temporary governing councils will be selected by the Spiritual Hierarchy.

To continue with the role of Planetary Advocate Groups in creating the emerging level of planetary consciousness, they will provide the space where consciousness can be explored despite the vast numbers of Earth humans.

This operation will be achieved through the use of fluid management. The role of PAGs is to link up with other groups who are to be a part of the consciousness-raising operation and expand the web of planetary consciousness to its fullest possible extent.

The unique nature of each PAG

As each group understands itself, works outward and begins connecting and networking with other groups, this process will create a natural increase in the web of consciousness. PAGs will share specific gifts or interests with other groups in order to generate enlightening insights and to demonstrate fluid management. Hence, each PAG has a specific purpose which it will develop.

Likewise, each PAG will have its own guardian angels, its own spiritual advisory groups — its own energy. Each PAG will then link with other spiritually-minded groups that likewise have their own energies, and they will discover how these many but quite similar energies can harmonize with one another. Planetary Advocate Groups will consequently use networking, joint meditations and rituals involving many groups to establish agreement between themselves and human society. For the most part, it is the re-creation of harmonic convergence writ large.

Rituals and the mass landings

I have mentioned rituals. We are going to provide ways of establishing harmony between Planetary Advocate Groups and our planetary society by means of large scale events. In this way, Planetary Advocate Groups are involved in creating a worldwide network of consciousness. They are using methods that groups can employ to get together and realize exactly what it is that they are doing. Additionally, they also see how these activities broaden their relationships with various other groups.

Before the mass landings, Planetary Advocate Groups will serve as beacons for the rising waves of consciousness on this planet. They are the nodes that take the group and individual energies and pass them along in networks of consciousness. PAGs will be the providers of information about the reasons for the Galactic Federation's mass landings.

There will be gatherings conducted between Planetary Advocate Groups so that they can remain highly informed. They will take the information they are given and bring it into their own gatherings. This is the forum concept on a large scale — people's forums meeting together to express consciousness, to express light-working, and to discern what it is that they are doing, because everyone has their own piece of the puzzle to add to this information.

The continuing process is, first of all, to enlarge (network) these personal and planetary energies and use this network to filter the energies in a meaningful and informative way. This is why I want to have all these gatherings followed with film or videotape, computer generated graphics et cetera, to allow each Planetary Advocate Group to perceive what is occurring.

As they participate in this activity, they will fully understand this ascension/transformation process. Individuals can then take what is given, through questioning and inner counseling, and come up with their own answers to give to the group. This proper use of discernment is a very important part of the whole process of realizing what is happening to us.

Summary

Planetary Advocate Groups will provide training for their members — procedures to be followed when the mass landings occur. All these groups will be given guidance in the entire set of procedures and how these landings are to established in specific areas. They will also be instructed in how the Life/Light Centers are to be centers for aiding people through the process of consciousness transformation and for passing on the specific instructions of the Galactic Federation — to be given at the appropriate time to aid this process of radical change.

After the mass landings, the Planetary Advocate Groups will assist the Galactic Federation initially by preparing members of society for full consciousness. Remember in my lectures I stated that the main project of the Galactic Federation was to bring us into full consciousness, and that this full consciousness would be achieved within one to six months after the landings. The job of the Planetary Advocate Groups is to act as the primary intermediary. Thus PAGs will serve as the local forum where Galactic Federation personnel and earth humans can easily interact.

The key point for all humans on this planet to comprehend is that they are all part of the process of rising consciousness and of the ascension of our civilization and our planet The Galactic Federation is here to assist us. The First Contact Team is going to give us information and allow us to use PAGs, meditation groups, Guardian groups, et cetera, to form a web of consciousness that will act as the great foundation upon which our new, fully conscious galactic civilization is to be created.

SEVEN
Some Final Comments

As I have been stating throughout this part of the book, Planetary Advocate Groups (PAGs) are the models that have been given to us by the Spiritual Hierarchy and the Galactic Federation. Their purpose is to serve as one of the major tools to help create the galactic civilization. In applying this instrument for change, we will be able to effect a constructive transformation of our planet and our society.

PAGs and society — an important connection

Planetary Advocate Groups are the basis for a worldwide network for consciousness and for our own and our planet's ascension process. They can teach us about ourselves and our society. For too long we have believed that rapid change was only possible with the aid and consent of our traditional local and national governments. Now is the time to end this mental and emotional bondage and allow ourselves to begin to create a galactic human society.

But, you may ask, how is this vast shift to occur? The answer lies in ourselves and our ability to make a commitment for change. Throughout this part of the book I have given you a means to effect this change and create a new reality. The key is to apply it now and to apply it on a worldwide basis. We have the privilege of being the first generations of Earth humans that will be able to move from limited consciousness to full consciousness. This gift is being given to us because we represent those proud, capable and creative souls that have volunteered for this immense and necessary project. We starseeds who have incarnated on this planet are the various ambassadors of a new reality.

This aspect has up till now been largely forgotten. The Earth is a vast amnesia zone and amnesia has crippled us for too long. Consequently, the Spiritual Hierarchy and the Ascended Masters have been changing our spiritual, physical and emotional perceptions. These changes, along with our own attempts at remembrance, have slowly begun to lift some of the thick fog that surrounds us.

As we begin to feel the new light of a transforming reality, we begin to perceive it at a deep emotional and physical level. This new conceptualization of ourselves and our world is being daily observed and noted by Earth's humanity. Yet few of us fully comprehend its significance. It is our task to deliver the wake-up call to our brothers and sisters and apprise them of what is truly happening around this planet.

For the planet has given us a timetable for these vital actions. The planet intends to fulfill its destiny and become a fully conscious life form by the end of 1996. This emergence gives us little time for action. So it is imperative that we act in as timely a manner as possible and the key to this commitment is our joy and our inner purpose.

What we have to do is put ourselves in a condition of centered self-purpose and use it for joyfully giving to others the gifts and abilities we possess. And be it known that all light workers have an immense reservoir of love, commitment and capability.

We have a great responsibility because of our capabilities. All of us, when we finally come together in a mighty planetary network, possess the different parts of the puzzle required to make this a most successful effort. What we now need to do is to support one another and use our joint energies to assure this calculated success.

Our responsibility is to come together in groups and form the foundation for Earth's new humanity. At present, the economic, social and governmental structures of this planet are slowly but assuredly failing. The planet's population is engaged in a vast and seemingly chaotic movement that appears to be provoking it towards self-destruction.

Yet this process is simply the final disbursement of national, regional and global karma that this wayward civilization has accumulated in its travels through history. The time to end this nonsense has now arrived and we as a planet have been thrown headlong into a new reality. But first there is the test of flames and it will be administered with love by the Spiritual Hierarchy. For the Spiritual Hierarchy realizes that we are here to overcome these difficulties and they are here to help us. This aid consists of raising our consciousness and giving us the tools to accomplish our mission.

Perhaps it is now time to state this mission fully and thereby allow you to comprehend its varied implications. In a nutshell, we are the 'grounding crew' for a new paradigm and a new civilization — a galactic human civilization. What does this really mean? It means that we have taken on the huge responsibility to signal our Earth human family that something wonderful is about to happen. But the mission is more than being harbingers for a new reality. We are here to perform two important tasks.

First, we must establish and organize a worldwide network of groups dedicated to helping us get out the message and, second, we then have to act as the prime assistants to the Spiritual Hierarchy, Ascended Masters and the Galactic Federation in the actual 'midwifing' of our planet's human population as it transforms into full consciousness. In short, we are among those to be processed and at the same time we are meant to be assistants to the processors. This is a most Herculean and yet miraculous task that we are about to perform.

As a result, all of us are expected to be able to put ourselves into a proper working order relatively quickly. This is because we have been chosen to bring ourselves quickly through our various mental, emotional and spiritual blocks. We need each other's support in our individual efforts to weave quickly through what we have accumulated in a lifetime.

For we are the examples of how this change in consciousness can be accomplished. This process makes it imperative that the PAGs be formed in joy and out of our own inner purposes — our talents, knowledge and creative capabilities. From this foundation we can then establish the initial parts of the immense mosaic that will be our new galactic civilization.

PAGs — a new mosaic of reality

This mosaic of a new perception of reality (the paradigm of ascension) creates a new karma and a new set of responsibilities for everyone. This new karma links us into the activity of being unique mirror images of ourselves — yet mirror images with a slight difference. Each one of our connected selves and realities will have a special aspect to contribute to the whole. It is as if we were special pieces of a hologram that could re-create the whole, but also has the capability to establish a special 'twist' on this whole. It is this aspect that waits in us to be reborn. It is also this aspect that waits for us to accept its presence.

So we have to use this ability and permit ourselves to achieve what now seems the impossible. We are on a journey to a new world and to a new series of realities. Both are a part of each other and create the means for learning more about ourselves as a guardian and as an aspect of our third-dimensional mastery.

This journey is, blessedly, a short one and hence one that signifies that much is expected from us in a very short time. Therefore let us use those tools given to us and allow them to achieve their full purposes, for we are the maestros of full consciousness. The Angelic guardians of this realm did choose us after much supplication and deliberation. Therefore, rejoice and use your capabilities, desires and — most of all — your inner intuitive purposes.

The time has come for action. Initially do what you can and then allow the miracle to happen. You will discover the wonders of this new reality as it rapidly spreads its wings and grows into an all-encompassing existence. But be kind to yourself and allow the natural process of change to occur.

A major part of this system is the process of 'fluid management'. Fluid management has the capability to develop the potential of every person. It can accomplish this by encouraging group interaction. It can also increase consciousness and allow this web or network of consciousness to create a galactic civilization. This civilization represents everything we have been talking about — it is based upon the divine plan that adapts itself to the needs and desires of the Spiritual Hierarchy of our planet and the Creator's plan.

Advocate groups will thus coordinate with the Spiritual Hierarchy and the Galactic Federation in creating this galactic civilization. The civilization is created according to a divine plan that was established long ago and is now being activated by the Creation. We are here to provide ourselves as the means for this glorious spiritual activation, which is the result of those activities performed by all of us during the course of the past six decades.

Planetary Advocate Groups are the foundation for establishing the various Life/Light Centers in all parts of this planet. What we will discover is that Light/Life Centers will have an energy about them. As they come together and especially as PAGs and affiliated groups interact with one another, they will discover that these centers are actually a series of Planetary Advocate Groups — Planetary Advocate Groups writ large with a special purpose.

This purpose will be determined by the very nature of the exchange between PAGs, affiliated groups and the Life/Light Centers. Thus Life/Light Centers and Planetary Advocate Groups will almost become a part of each other. This process is an example of how our consciousness is merging yet maintaining a degree of difference. It is this seeming anomaly that drives the new consciousness and the new galactic society.

Firstly, Planetary Advocate Groups are a way to find out about the new galactic civilization. Consequently, Planetary Advocate Groups are also a way for allowing all of us to experience the dynamics of fluid management and to learn a new way of managing groups. This technique is one of the most important aspects of the new galactic civilization. For, by following this new organizing system, we will be able to understand and interact with one another as fully conscious beings — beings who have a meaningful, purposeful and very high concept of who and what we are.

Secondly, PAGs are providing the nodes, as I have stated, for developing the web of consciousness that is essential for creating the new galactic civilization. This new civilization is based upon individuals interacting with one another on both the local and the planetary level. These are the two basic interaction points. We are going to learn how to interact easily at these two points. Right now it may seem very difficult, but it will be done.

Planetary Advocate Groups consist of interconnected humans who support and maintain the web of consciousness. This web of consciousness consists simply of the combined energies of every human on the planet, our fellow cetaceans and the Spiritual Hierarchy. We are going to provide our contribution to this important spiritual and guardian energy, which will help to maintain it, since the physical is the key point at which maintenance of this web is accomplished.

Summary

In summation, Planetary Advocate Groups are the key to creating a new galactic civilization because they are the training units for providing us with the energies and the knowledge of how the new galactic society operates. Planetary Advocate Groups practice the principles of 'fluid management' and support the developing worldwide network of consciousness.

We have explained how this 'fluid management' aids the consciousness. It allows us to be creative. 'Fluid management' gives every human being a way to express his or her own creative energies and use those talents to create a greater spiritual energy — a synergy, we might call it, of third-dimensional reality and multidimensional consciousness.

Most importantly, PAGs assist the Spiritual Hierarchy and the Galactic Federation in making the mass landings a success. PAGS and the Life/Light Centers provide the Earth human link to the whole new reality (paradigm of ascension). Without that link, this vast shift in consciousness cannot be so easily put into place on this planet.

Consciousness on this planet has been given to all of us in full measure for one purpose, so that we can become the people we are meant to be — spiritual and physical beings who are here to help create a true energy of guardianship. These true energies are the ones that in turn allow this planet to successfully become what it is meant to be — a fully conscious life form.

To keep in touch with the latest news and developments, see VictoryNet Website at
http://www.victory-net.com/
It is also possible to join the VictoryNet Round Table — see Resources section at end of book.

Sheldon Nidle

Sheldon Nidle was born in New York City on November 11, 1946 and grew up in Buffalo, New York. His first extraterrestrial (ET) and UFO experiences began in 1955 with various modes of phenomena and contact manifestations, e.g. Light form phenomena, extraterrestrial visitations, teaching sessions, telepathic communications, and direct core knowledge inserts. He has had numerous craft sightings throughout the years.

At about 14 years old, Sheldon demanded that the ETs stop communicating with him because he felt that their knowledge ran counter to contemporary scientific reasoning. They left but told him they would be back. In high school, he was in advanced science programs such as physics, chemistry and calculus. As a teenager, he was part of a team that invented the field ion microscope. As an undergraduate at the State University of New York at Buffalo, he was vice president of the Amateur Astronomers' Club.

Sheldon's vision is for people to be activated in service to create a cooperative web of consciousness for the new galactic civilization. His mission is to establish international Planetary Advocate Groups and to inform and educate us regarding the changes that are occurring (our accelerated shift into full consciousness) and our new roles as galactic humans.

Education
M.A. in Southeast Asian Government
M.A. in American Politics & International Public Administration
University of Southern California Ph.D. candidate (1974-6)

Occupation
Representative and lecturer for the Galactic Federation, and co-author of the best-seller *You Are Becoming a Galactic Human* (June 1994). In the 1970s he was vice-president for scientific programming for Syntar Productions, where he created a documentary on the life and accomplishments of Nikola Tesla, the genius who invented the technology of the 20th century. Throughout the 70s up to the mid-80s he was involved in scientific research on alternative sources of electrical energy. In the mid-80s his ET contacts reappeared and subsequently led him to the information presented through his books, lectures and videos.

Part Two

Entering the New Time

Creation of Planetary Calendar Councils and a Planet Art Network

José Argüelles

"Time is the fourth dimension," declared Albert Einstein. But he could say little more about it, for he did not know that the fourth dimension is governed by a mathematics entirely different from the mathematics of third-dimensional space. V.I. Vernadsky, indefatigable pioneer of the laws and science of the biosphere, declared again and again toward the end of his life (1944) that our knowledge of the biosphere was complete in all but one respect: an accurate understanding of the laws of time. Vernadsky knew that we are handicapped by the fact that what we think of as time is actually the application of the laws of space to time. As a result we do not know time at all and our species, through uncontrolled biological expansion of its own mass as well as of the machines it produces, has now exceeded its own proportion and is in the process of destroying the biosphere altogether.

The Fourth Dimension:
Qualities and Nature of Time

1. Just as air is the atmosphere of the body, so time is the atmosphere of the mind. If the time in which we live consists of uneven months and days regulated by mechanized minutes and hours, that is what becomes of our mind: a mechanized irregularity. Since everything follows from mind, it is no wonder that the atmosphere in which we live daily becomes more polluted, and the greatest complaint is: "I just don't have enough time!" Whoever owns your time, owns your mind Own your own time and you will know your own mind.

2. There are two essential characteristics of time, which is the fourth dimension: mental and aesthetic. Time is mental because it is experienced and known through the mind. Mental cultivation is basic to the experience of time. Time is aesthetic because it consists of different whole levels of order whose proportions and ratios are consistent across scale, each level or order of which is reflected holographically in every other. Aesthetic contemplation and artistic activity are the object and expressive reflex of time. As mind is the root of time, the sensory ratios of artistic experience are the expression of time.

Because of its unconscious immersion in the third-dimensional level of space, which is commonly known as the material plane, the subcorpus humanity as a species or collective whole has not yet understood or risen to the level of conscious fourth-dimension operation. Unconscious participation in the fourth dimension is common through dreams and related states as well as the varieties of often barely tolerated artistic expression. The experience of time as the fourth dimension does not deny but enhances and gives ordered context to the sensual experience of the third dimension.

3. The fourth dimension is frequently associated with the after-

death state. It may be asked: Is it not a contradiction to speak of the living experience of time as the fourth dimension, and yet speak of the fourth dimension in reference to the after-death state? There is no contradiction. Much as space penetrates all solids, time as the fourth dimension permeates the living as well as the pre-birth and post-mortem states of being which extend beyond the living corpus.

Within the realm of the physical plane or third dimension, the permeation of time is known and experienced as 'the now'. There is only one now, and at the same time there are an infinite number of nows for an infinite number of beings. This now moment, which is without measure and intangible, experienced through mind but capable of accelerating nervous excitation and awareness through all of the senses, is no different than the gateway experience opening into the post-mortem state. It is true that there is a realm of fourth-dimensional experience existing apart from the daily experience of the third-dimensional body. Yet this realm can be accessed through the cultivation of the mind in the now. The fundamental technique for cultivating this state of nowness is referred to as 'Practicing the Universal Equality of Awareness' (see Chapter 13).

4. From the point of view of the fourth dimension, the distinctions made between the living and the non-living are functions of the dualism of mind fostered by exclusive reliance on methods of third-dimensional science, which further reinforce already-existing erroneous thought patterns fixed in unexamined beliefs regarding 'life' and 'death'. Once the art and science of fourth-dimensional time are properly understood and practiced, common current third-dimensional beliefs, distinctions and practices regarding life and death will alter greatly.

5. Space is materially or sensually tangible, time is mentally tangible. Space is the third dimension. Time is the fourth dimension. In relation to space, time is intangible and immeasurable. In relation to time, space is an infinitely locatable point. Though time may be intangible and immeasurable by the third-dimensional standards of space which are finite and self-limiting, within the standards of the fourth dimension, time has its structures which, being infinite, are defined by ratios and proportions rather than by limiting

equations and geometries of forms. These ratios and proportions of fourth-dimensional time will be dealt with in their entirety following the chronomantic description of the three universal whole orders.

6. The three universal wholes given order by fourth-dimensional time are the galactic, the stellar and the planetary. Each of these orders is a holographic projection of the others. Time as the fourth dimension moves from the largest-scale whole to the smallest. The largest-scale whole is the galaxy or galactic order. What we experience astrophysically through our eyes and third-dimensional instrumentation is merely the physical aspect or outer garment of the galactic whole. As a multitude of subsets of different star systems which nonetheless retain a resonant relation to each other and to the whole, the galactic order itself is maintained by the fourth-dimensional ordering principle of time. The typical spiral form of the galaxy is an aesthetic third-dimensional reflection of the fourth-dimensional ordering system of time which is infinitely aesthetic and mental in origin and nature.

The descriptions of ultimate origins and endings (big bangs and black holes) are merely projections of the third-dimensional mind immersed in its dualistic belief in maintaining a distinction between life and death. Time as the fourth dimension is without beginning or end. There are only cycles within cycles within cycles. Cycles merely define levels and stages of impermanence, which is the chief characteristic of all physical-plane third-dimensional phenomena. The planetary cycle is contained within the stellar cycle; the stellar cycle is contained within the galactic cycle; the galactic cycle is contained within the universal whole; the universal whole is a self-created, self-sustaining mental creation beyond our present capacity to fathom.

7. Planet Earth is not a spaceship, but a timeship. A spaceship, defined as an object following a trajectory in space, nonetheless experiences and is limited by time. No matter how 'far' the spaceship is thought to travel, it cannot escape the variables of time which condition its impermanence. Even 'immobility' experiences time. All any third-dimensional object can do is maintain its own space.

Even a spaceship sailing through space must maintain its own objectified space. A spaceship travels in space. Its capacities are finite; its goals self-limited. A timeship travels in time. Its capacities are infinite; its goals immeasurable.

A spaceship supporting life is further limited by its finite space to a threshold of propagation and multiplication of species beyond which there can only be three choices: stasis, self-destruction, biomutation.

A planet is a single object moving in its own space. Rotating on its own power a planet maintains its own space as a spiralling orbit around a stellar body. Through resonance with its stellar order, a planet becomes a timeship. A timeship maintains its space in order to afford a conscious experience of the infinite ratios and cycles of time. If the chief characteristics or qualities of time are the mental and the aesthetic, a planetary timeship is one possessing an intelligence capable of crafting itself into a mentally conceived and projected whole aesthetic order or system. This is possible because time is a superior mental order that encompasses and moves through the three universal levels or wholes — the galactic, the stellar and the planetary.

Through conscious self-reflection, the experience of the smallest whole, the planetary, the other two levels, stellar and galactic, can be holographically experienced and known. A planetary timeship presupposes a type of biosphere capable of transforming itself into a noosphere, and a noosphere capable of manifesting a psi bank. The existence of a psi bank itself presupposes an intelligent intentionality existing at a level beyond and preceding the evolution of the noosphere and psi bank, and capable of instrumenting a universal memory field to be released in different stages through the galactic timing frequency, 13:20.

8. The fourth-dimensional body of a planetary timeship is known as the holon. The holon is the term given to the whole order or structure of fourth-dimensional time, be it at the galactic, stellar or planetary levels. Each holon at each level possesses the same fractal ratios and properties, and hence a common field of resonance can be established from the planetary to the galactic levels. The structure of the planetary holon, which may be thought of as the

fourth-dimensional skeleton of the planet, is an icosahedral or 20-sided pattern. Each of these 20 sides or facets is in actuality a tetrahedral form. Reduced to its essentials, any holon has as its underlying structure the tetrahedron, the primary and quintessential geometric form.

As the galactic level is the sum of a subset of star systems, and the stellar level is the sum of a subset of planetary systems, so the planetary system is the biogenic sum of a subset of interacting species and inert orders. In all three whole levels, the interacting subsets create and are determined by fields of resonance. A field of resonance may be understood either unconsciously or consciously. Ultimately the making conscious of a planetary field of resonance is a matter of free will. That is, the question of transforming a biosphere into a noosphere is a matter of choice of the intelligence of the dominant planetary species. To make this choice is to activate the holon or planetary timeship, to transform the biosphere into the noosphere, and to bring into conscious manifestation the psi bank.

9. The chronosphere is the fourth-dimensional field created by a planet holon in resonance with the rotation of the third-dimensional planet body. The basic fourth-dimensional unit of the chronosphere is the kin, the planetary standard of time which corresponds to the duration of a single rotation of the axis, one day-and-night. A single day-and-night rotation, or kin, is the registration of one biospheric pulsation of a single whole organism, planet. Since a kin is a fourth-dimensional unit, its holographic properties are infinite. In this way, though a kin is the registration of but a single biospheric pulsation, due to its holographically resonant properties the information contained within a kin may be infinitely expansive and holographically all-inclusive.

Through the pulsation of sequences of kin, defined by the 260 units of the fourth-dimensional galactic spin (see below), the planetary chronosphere is the encapsulating form which contains the information-bearing properties of the psi bank. As the fourth-dimensional form in time of the planetary holon, the chronosphere extends from the planetary core outward 40,000 miles, encompassing the magnetic sheath. The chronosphere is the information constant holding the psi bank in place within the noosphere. The form and pattern of the psi bank conforms to the daily and cyclic galactic patterning of the chronosphere.

Through duration in its space, the chronosphere builds up its information or free energy in geometrical progression, corresponding both to the evolution and expansion of the planetary living matter, and to the ecologically impactful and biogeological transformation of the human species within the planetary whole system. Such a build-up of unutilized and hence unconscious information/energy can be catalyzed at the biospheric-noospheric transition point to assist in the rapid mutation of the species and, indeed, of the entire ecosphere so that the psi bank may manifest and the next evolutionary level be easily attained. Once the planetary noosphere and the psi bank are activated, the chronosphere becomes self-regulating, so that the planet itself may evolve into a consciously realized aesthetic whole.

10. The free energy accumulated by the chronosphere is referred to as g-force or the fifth force. A planet consciously in time renews itself on g-force. It is the infinitely renewable galactic energy source. The g-force is the medium of the galactic synchronization beams, which themselves appear in accord with galactic timing codes. Available g-force increases with the increase of synchronization of the single planetary biospheric organism, kin after kin. The g-force is the transmutative energy which facilitates interdimensional interaction and reciprocity. Fourth-dimensional energy is fourth-dimensional information. The study and comprehension of the varieties of these transmutative interactions is referred to as chronobiology.

11. Chronobiology as it is presently understood refers to the study of time on living systems, especially rhythms and cycles. From the perspective of time in its own dimension, chronobiology refers to the interdimensional extension of conscious living third-dimensional forms into their fourth-dimensional correspondences. Chronogeology, likewise, refers to the study of the planet extended into the rhythms and patterns of the fourth dimension. Just as a third-dimensional planet has its fourth-dimensional holon and

chronosphere, so the third-dimensional human unit has its fourth-dimensional holon and chronosphere. The realization of the planet whole systems evolutionary future requires that the fulfillment of the human species come about through the equal fulfillment of each third-dimensional unit in conscious relation with its fourth-dimensional holon. As the individual becomes more collective, the collective becomes more individual. The communion of individual holons is attained in the total identification of the individual holon units with the planet holon. This condition is referred to as 'Universal Transcension'.

At present the human race is almost universally unconscious of the exact relation of its body to its holon, and chronobiology is at best at a primitive stage of development. However, in the present knowledge of DNA coding combined with environmental aesthetics and release from the 12:60 timing frequency, the field of chronobiology may rapidly advance. In essence, while the DNA code recognizes 64 codons and 20 utilizable amino acids, the chronobiological code encompasses these third-dimensional biological building blocks within a 260-unit galactic enzyme code referred to as 'galactic signatures'. Within the chronosphere, the 260 galactic enzymes or signatures are 'fed' by the g-force and this is the energy available to humans who assume their galactic signatures and become planetary kin. Since the psi bank contains the registrations of the 260 enzymes, the human unit as planetary kin has the opportunity for creative interaction with the psi bank and can become a factor in bringing about its conscious activation.

12. Chronomancy is the science and art of fourth-dimensional time considered as a whole system where science is knowledge and art is practice. Chronomancy has specific application as an intrinsically divinatory and oracular comprehension of events set within the holographic framework of the interdimensional information system which connects the three levels: galactic, stellar, planetary.

Oracular is used here in the sense of an authoritative communication whose information is immediately applicable. Divinatory refers to the process of direct intuitive perception by which the oracular communication is obtained. Because of the discovery of the mathematical proofs of the fourth dimension as well as their demonstration through an empirical form made universally available as the Dreamspell codes of galactic time, the divinatory oracular method of chronomancy is not one that can be usurped by a priesthood or an elite, as has been the case with all historical knowledge systems inclusive of 12:60 science. Rather, it is for each human as an autonomous unit in relation to its holon to chronomantically divine and to know for itself. The realization of this condition of human autonomy, which has the profoundest social, political and cultural ramifications, represents the next evolutionary advancement, and indeed fulfillment of the species *homo sapiens*.

From the 12:60 perspective, time as a mental construct is a system of sequential terms for determining the relationships which any event has to an arbitrarily conceived 'past' or 'future'. In this conception time is a linear model, the self-reinforcing product of a strictly deterministic mental attitude, profoundly conditioned by a dualistic belief in the absoluteness of life and death. Chronology is then little more than a process of dating events within an arbitrarily conceived scale of sequential relationships. In this mental construct, what is gone is dead, and what is to come is unknown. Prediction is given validity to the degree that it bases itself on known data derived from the narrow confines of this sequential linear mental construct. For this reason 12:60 prediction is little more than the tendency to project accelerated versions of itself by terms of geometrical progression into a future increasingly crowded by further technological 'solutions'.

By contrast, chronomancy operates from a superior fourth-dimensional mental construct in which time is known and experienced as a radial matrix: a self-existing system of ratios which govern the rhythms of living matter as well as of all celestial bodies, stars, galaxies and planets, in relation to themselves and to each other. As is demonstrated by the planet body Earth in its rotation on its own axis and its orbit around its local star, time is in the nature of a cyclical vortex. Within this cyclical vortex there are repeatable sequences or rounds of days or kin. To describe the rounds of days or kin as linear goes totally against the intrinsic spin and rotational power of the planet. Within this cyclical vortex (a galactic spin) there is a set of informational time event constants causing each day to differ from every other day, and yet endowing each day with qualities similar to other days within the set of rounds. Since the spin of the cyclical vortex is fractal and holographic in nature, the system of 'time events', though fixed and patterned, is not deterministic but contains infinite levels of accessible information.

From this it follows that there are chronomantic procedures for divining in an oracular manner the different levels of meaning and information from the fixed set of cyclical time events in order to establish ever greater levels of resonance and harmony between the human mind, its sensory ratios and the planetary environment. Were it not for the discovery of the mathematical proofs and demonstrations of the fourth dimension, the topic of chronomancy would be just another theory. Instead, with the understanding and application of the principles of time as the fourth dimension, chronomancy will be established and flourish widely, giving new life to third-dimensional space science which, reconstructed within the whole systems context, will be known as biogeomancy, the science and art of planetary knowing.

From *A Treatise on Time Viewed from Its Own Dimension*

TWO

Mathematical Principles of Fourth-Dimensional Time

Radial Matrix

The fourth dimension is mathematically constructed as a radial matrix. A radial matrix is a self-existing order of number ratios and harmonics whose units and proportions are generated radially, and of which, in part and in sum, all of the units possess a radial relation to each other. All fourth-dimensional mathematics are radial; all radial matrices are whole number sets. There are no irrational or fractional numbers, but instead simple sets of fractals and ratios whose power of exponential magnification is infinite.

In its formulaic essence the radial matrix is demonstrated as the 0-19 galactic notational code. In this code, as in any radial matrix, there are equal orders of simultaneous sets extending from an infinite and indefinable centerpoint and extending equally in all directions. Each order of sets consists at minimum of two equally extended antipodal orders, and the sums of all sets of antipodal orders, represented by a set of numbers and their subsets independent of the antipodal orders, is equal, e.g. in the 0-19 code, the sum is always 19.

The totality of radial sets of antipodal orders and the number sets from which they are constructed is referred to as a matrix, the underlying self-generated order of time as the fourth dimension. Because the mathematical description of the matrix underlying order of the fourth dimension is radiative and reciprocally self-informing in all its parts, time cannot properly be conceived of as linear, nor can it be said to have any beginning or end point.

Fractals

Fourth-dimensional radial mathematical constructs describing energetic and informational transformations are purely fractal in nature, even where types of geometry are involved. Fractals are self-existing, holographic and infinitely scalar, maintaining their proportions over any magnitude of scale. Fractals are to the fourth dimension what geometry is to the third dimension. For third-dimensional science there is no space without matter and energy; however, time has always been open to question, for as Vernadsky points out, 'time is not a dimension of metric geometry'.

Third-dimensional space-matter science is built up of geometries which describe a world of solids of varying degrees of complexity, while algebraic equations are used to describe the energetic transformations of the different elemental states spanning the ever-changing world of the solids. Time cannot be described in this way, nor can it really be said to be described vectorally.

However, from the perspective of the fourth dimension, space may either be an infinitely locatable point, or a single point supplied by an infinitesimal vector. The single point in space conforms to the now moment for any number of infinite orders of being capable of experiencing the now at any given point in space. This infinitely locatable point of space may be informed by series of fractals whose proportions yield different forms of information. This information is in the nature of interactive timing frequencies. The timing frequencies are results of different levels of ratio downloads which are understood as information governing different stages of evolutionary whole systems change.

The fractal series available to any given moment or set of moments pertaining to the infinitely locatable point in space are always dependent on variables of evolutionary stage, mental development and self-reflective awareness.

From this two corollaries are to be drawn: timing frequencies and time itself are understandable only from a whole systems approach; and until there is a self-reflective capacity of mental development, the science of time cannot be properly elaborated upon. Conversely, the entrainment of mind to the nature of the fourth-dimensional matrix and the fractals which are facilitated by this matrix open the mind to its further evolution. In other words, we cannot speak of timing frequencies and the fractals of time without speaking of the mind's evolutionary advancement.

The timing frequencies themselves, in relation to the phenomena of the third dimension, are holographically inclusive and extend from larger and more inclusive levels of order to lesser levels of order. Though it is a truism to speak of the inseparability of space and time, or of the space-time continuum, in truth time is the ordering principle of space, and only as the container of space (and not vice versa) can it be said to be inseparable from space. Though in no way can time be described from the exclusive formulae of third-dimensional science and mathematics, fourth-dimensional mathematics can supply new synthesizing levels of understanding for dealing with the matter-energy permutations of third-dimensional space.

In fourth-dimensional order a number is not a quantitative function but a qualitative composite, a precise intersection of fractal possibilities whose different harmonic and chromatic textures open the mind to its own sensorium. The different fractal ratios of fourth-dimensional time consist of moving sums of number relations. The resonant interaction of these moving number relations constitutes the palpable mental medium of the radial matrix. The different sets of fractal ratios nested infinitely within each other define the equally infinite levels of creative order unceasingly generated by the matrix.

The key fourth-dimensional fractal unit is known as the wavespell, which is defined as a self-existing 13-unit (kin) cosmology. The key number units involved in the constituent creation of the 13-kin wavespell are: 4, a composite of the first three orders of number, which establishes the self-existing order; 5 (4+1), which brings in the overtone power of the g-force; and 13 (4+5+4), which is the cosmic tone informing the fifth; between the fifth (4+1) and the thirteenth (9+4) orders is the 8, the logarithmic fractal interval between the 5 and the 13 (5+3=8, 8+5=13). Hence the key wavespell ratio: 5:8 :: 8:13.

Ratios

Just as the geometries of the third dimension yield descriptions of solids in all of their energetic fluctuations, even if these solids are merely sub-atomic particles, so the fractals of the fourth dimension yield different sets of ratios which inform the timing frequencies at all levels of operation. The ratios are dependent upon and coordinated by the number orders of the radial matrix, and provide the informative content of the different fractals. Ultimately, the ratios describe both the different capacities of the timing frequencies and the sensory orders of human experience.

The mathematical ratios whose proportions remain constant across scale create fractal equivalences with themselves in different magnitudes of scale or with other sets of ratios. In the wavespell example, the constituent ratio, 5:8 :: 8:13, remains constant whether the kin unit of the wavespell is the equivalent of a day, a moon, a year etc. Like number, all ratios are mental in nature and are complemented or augmented by analogical orders of metaphor. Just as mind is the sub- and superstratum of reality, so the fourth dimension is the sub- and superstratum of the third dimension.

The mental order or condition of time is no less real or unreal than the traditional solid, liquid and gaseous states of the third dimension. As a mental order, time and the fourth dimension are an all-encompassing and all-permeating state or condition, superseding the physiochemical liquid, solid and gaseous states, while informing the full spectrum of electromagnetic energy transitions perceptible as the third dimension. In other words, as the sum of the ratio expressions of the galactic mental order, time is in actuality the origin of the third-dimensional physiochemical changes, their agent of transmutation, and their noospheric transformational conclusion.

In the full development of the pulsar science of the wavespell in all of its ratio permutations is to be found the full fourth-dimensional complement of the third-dimensional biophysical and geochemical sciences. The 'scale' of ratios is provided by the 'Harmonic Index' which displays the full range of the 260-kin permutations defining the galactic interdimensional enzymes, as well as the 32 binary sets of harmonics by which time as galactic biology orders itself into a self-organizing system of four-unit microwholes called harmonics.

The Tetrahedron and Tetrahedral Order

The tetrahedron, the primal geometric form found naturally in crystalline states, is the agent of information and energy transductions between the third and fourth dimensions. From the fourth dimension the tetrahedron facilitates ratio energy transduction into third-dimensional quanta; from the third dimension, the tetrahedron facilitates the transduction of quantum information into fourth-dimensional energy, which is spectral rather than material in nature. Fourth-dimensional spectral phenomena are characterized by form and luminosity but lack volume and mass.

As the formal organizing unit of the fourth dimension, the structure of the tetrahedron underlies and informs the wavespell's ratios and pulsar 'geometries'. To each of the four points of the tetrahedron correspond the first, fifth, ninth and thirteenth positions of the wavespell. The unity in time of these four wavespell positions conditions the fourth-dimensional properties of the tetrahedron. The three remaining sets of three units each of the wavespell establish three interactive, triangular planes of time joined by a common point. This point is the invisible fifth or 'plus one' center point of the interior of the tetrahedron from which extend four vertices ending at each of the tetrahedron's four visible points. This center point also represents the g-force ratio conduit between the infinitely locatable point of third-dimensional space — the now — and the higher fourth- and fifth-dimensional orders of galactic time and mind.

Tetrahedral order refers to the use of the tetrahedron in the description and construction of other holon forms, for example the icosahedral planet holon. In actuality all classic geometrical forms are tetrahedral derivatives; likewise the core and structure of the Earth as a solid are crystalline in origin and in the nature of a complex tetrahedral order. Just as the ultimate geometrical reduction of quanta is a tetrahedron, so the minimum condensation of fourth-dimensional information is also a tetrahedron. As the sum of all formal geometrical possibilities, the sphere contains the tetrahedron at its core.

The Plus One Factor

The plus one (+1) factor is the mathematical principle of the recirculation of time as a spiral vortex. Without the plus one factor, there would be a flat stasis, a constantly re-recorded musical score with a forgotten beginning and an unwanted ending, at best resolved into the kind of hopelessly complex entropic order which third-dimensional human civilization now exhibits. The plus one factor transforms a moving orbit on a flat plane in space into a vortex in time.

Plus one represents the overtone power of the g-force (4+1). In terms of relativity, the formula for time is stated: T=f (E=MC² +1). Time is a function of the speed of light plus one; properly put, light is overtoned by time. By bringing in the overtone, the interdimensional g-force resonance, the plus one factor places any third-dimensional phenomenon measurable by third-dimensional instrumentation, even light, into its immeasurable and intangible fourth-dimensional condition where mutation is a realizable option.

In the dot-bar galactic 0-19 code, the plus one factor is represented as the passage from the four dot equivalence of the number four, or the order of the fourth, to the bar equivalence of five or the order of the fifth. In the color formula of the time harmonics, red-white-blue-yellow, the plus one factor yields the fifth color, green, resulting in a fifth time cell. In the tetrahedron, the three sides automatically create a plus one, the fourth side; while the four points tacitly proceed from a fifth interior point, the plus one factor holding the tetrahedron together.

The plus one factor is the power of time to transmute complex forms beyond their point of entropic stasis. While 12 is a complex number of a crystalline yet static perfection, plus one yields 13, the prime number representing the galactic power of the vortical recirculation of time. Likewise the 32 sets of binary Harmonics yield 64, matching the set of 64 DNA codons, which like the complex 12, yields a stasis; 64 plus one, the unpaired 33rd Harmonic, yields 65 (13 x 5), representing the interdimensional power of the g-force to invigorate the corpus of living matter beyond itself into its next evolutionary stage.

Thirteen perfect moons of 28 days each yields 364. Like 12, 32 and 64, 364 is an even more complex number also represented as 52 x 7, the number of weeks in a solar year; 364 plus one, green day, which is outside of the days of the calendar, yields 365 (5 x 73), the number of whole days in the Earth's solar orbit, thus assuring the 13-moon cycle the power of vortical recirculation. This power of recirculation is demonstrated by the fact that the solar-galactic year follows the ever-changing harmonic sequence of red, white, blue and yellow years.

Summary

The mathematical principles of the fourth dimension governing time and the timing frequencies of orders of whole systems are:

i) radial, hence consisting of radically non-linear, harmonic sets of matching whole number patterns operating as

ii) a matrix, a self-existing and self-generating whole number construct whose power of movement is

iii) fractal, whole number configurations capable of symmetrical consistency across scale; fractals are constructed of

iv) ratios, which bear information through sets of constant proportions;

v) the tetrahedron is the minimal geometrical form with maximum information-bearing capacity; while

vi) the plus one factor resolves all stasis and assures continuous recirculation of information as a vortex continuum without beginning or end.

From *A Treatise on Time Viewed from Its Own Dimension*

THREE

Mind and the Noosphere

At present, the belief system of the 12:60 mental field has created an artificial, yet totally illusory, mental shield around the planet. The rigidity of this belief system is all that keeps humanity not only from realizing that the chronosphere exists but also from receiving the enormous benefits of its presence. The 12:60 planetary mental shield is sustained by an artificial feedback loop which is a self-reinforcing system. At the root of this artificial 12:60 system is the belief that time is linear. To accept this belief is to surrender one's free will, for the belief that time is linear consigns the believer into a mental trap that says there is no choice but to go ahead according to the available options, which have all been conditioned by a linear development that can have only one foregone conclusion. In addition to contradicting the facts of the Earth's rotational momentum, spin and orbital circulation, the fatalism of the belief that time is linear generates a mental disease that afflicts all of humanity and the planet without exception.

This mental disease manifests in the order of reality as it is known today, one governed by the principle 'time is money'. The inescapable power of this 12:60 order of reality is referred to as Atlantis Corporation — 'Atlantis' because the very name conjures an amnesiac grandeur and 'corporation' because of the tendency to incorporate everything into a material form that can be exchanged for and/or be valued by money. This is the essence of the 12:60 mental disease, a genuine memory virus that manifests as the artificial planetary mental shield of global materialism.

Yet being artificial the 12:60 mental shield cannot withstand the overpowering effects of the g-force, the natural self-existing 13:20 galactic timing frequency. As the tide of the 13:20 timing frequency washes back in, the 12:60 timing frequency diminishes in power and, like a sandbar occasioned at one moment by perturbations in the geomagnetism affecting the ocean swells, in another moment it is gone again, swallowed by the vast ocean of galactic time. Once it is evident that the 12:60 is merely a rapidly eroding illusion, a lesser sandbar of consciousness, then the election of the collective human will to the higher order of reality will become the easier course.

Since the chronosphere operates at a regular 13:20 frequency, once humanity is consciously operating on the 13:20 frequency via acceptance of the 13-moon calendar, then the entire three-part field regulated by the chronosphere will come into resonance with itself. Being in resonance with itself, it will bring forth its own 13:20 mantle of mind — the noosphere — to be activated as the psi bank, the information code that places the third and fourth dimensions in synchronization with each other. The Dreamspell is the set of tools to unlock the psi bank and, in so doing, to evoke the Dreamspell user's own imminent enlightenment. Unlike the artificially generated 12:60 feedback loop, which is like bad air continuously circulated within a closed system, the 13:20 chronospheric feedback loop is galactic in nature and origin. The chronosphere's free operation assures its own illumination.

For humanity, the crux and nexus of this evolutionary shift toward whole illumination — universal transcension — is the need to tend properly to the biosphere. As the biopsychic field, the description of the biosphere is inclusive of its transition into the noosphere. What this means is the conscious interpenetration of the fourth dimension into the third dimension, the evolutionary advancement of the Dreamspell codes into a co-creative unlocking of the memory-generating patterns governing the Earth's own whole systems development. Again, once humanity releases itself from the grip of the artificial 12:60 timing frequency, the flood gates will open.

According to the Dreamspell analysis and critique, humanity is genetically in the driver's seat and has the capacity to bring about the conscious resonance of the three fields of the chronosphere: the electromagnetic, the biopsychic and the gravitational. Through the application of the Dreamspell codes, the human subcorpus of planetary living matter can exert a creative synthesis whereby the electromagnetic field is psychophysically reconstituted through the senses; the biopsychic field is reorganized as the telepathic cosmic order of human society indistinguishable from the living orders of nature; and the gravitational field is brought to a new level of balance through a vibrant correlation and symbiosis of the two third-dimensional geochemical orders SO_2 (silicon dioxide) and CO_2 (carbon dioxide). As far-fetched as this geochemical correlation may seem initially, it is founded on the holon congruence of the different levels and functions of the biosphere considered as an evolving form of time.

The effective method for bringing about this gravitational synthesis of social and geochemical order is to be found in the harmonization of the two orders of biospheric reality presented by the third-dimensional SO_2 and CO_2 molecular programs. The SO_2 silicon dioxide order of reality represents the 'inert' corpus of the Earth's biosphere, and the key underlying matrix of Earth's dense physical core. CO_2, the carbon dioxide cycle, is the base of the program sustaining the corpus of living matter, or biomass, from the photosynthesis of plants to the respiration of the human organism.

As SO_2, the quartz crystal represents a maximally radial simplification of form with a maximum increase of transduction capacity — the power to change one state of energy into another.

As the key genetic component of the CO_2 cycle, the human represents a maximally radial complexification of form with a maximum increase in sentiency — the power to absorb new feeling states in full self-reflective absorbency. Both crystal and human are complete resonators of the radial matrix. A future, yet immediately realizable, means for accelerating the evolution of the biosphere into the noosphere is to be found in this simple symbiotic translation: the unfathomed ranges of human sentiency applied by mental means to crystal transduction. In this way the advent of the noosphere is prepared, the evolution of the biosphere into expanded states of transductive sentiency opening to untold possibilities of sentient transduction. One chronosphere, one planet, one interdependent spectrum of evolutionary possibilities: the realization of the harmonic convergence of the SO_2 and CO_2 cycles will open vistas to the creation of the planet art spore.

Operating as the internalization of the three fields of resonance, and allowing the socially reorganizing capacity of the Dreamspell codes to impact on their own perceptions, humans will liberate untold amounts of psychic energy now long pent up within the artificial 12:60 mental shield. The release of these energies, creatively moderated by the planetary service wavespell of the 13-

Moon Calendar, will bring about the telepathic reorganization of human society.

But first humanity must use the new calendar to come to terms with its own belief in money as a value. The 13-moon restructuring of this belief will result in planetary programs to equalize the current status of wealth. With the reordering of concepts of wealth mandated by the new calendar, existing political forms will also be streamlined and used to create an orderly transition out of the 12:60 institutional realm and back into nature. This return to the natural order will be opened up first of all by a concerted effort to clean up and restore the environment, followed by realization of the laws unifying the human mental experience with the larger timing frequency governing nature, the 13:20.

The sum of these early efforts at self-reorganization according to the new calendar and re-entry into the proper timing frequency will establish humanity in an accelerated evolutionary trajectory. Understanding at last the nature of time, living at last in time with nature, humanity will know time as advancement into sensory mental realms of experience only enhanced by the telepathic capacity to know as one and to penetrate and enter whatever needs to be known. Since time is biology, and biology is art, in this tuning of the human into its own natural timing frequency lies the capacity for the whole system Earth to attain its evolutionary resolution as a planetary art spore. More than this I cannot say, for my vision is only my vision. It is for the intelligence of the entire collective corpus humanity to make the choice it has to make.

As I stated at the outset, science is an evolutionary phenomenon. When the programs by which we live are no longer anything more than orders of self-maintenance, the laws by which our own evolution and self-reflection are governed are to be discovered or even invented anew.

From *13 Moons in Motion*

FOUR

Thinking About the Unthinkable

Of all the unexamined assumptions and criteria upon which we base and gauge our daily lives as human beings on planet Earth, by far the greatest and most profoundly unquestioned is the instrument and institution known as the Gregorian calendar.

A calendar — any calendar — is commonly understood as a system for dividing time over extended periods. A day is the base unit of a calendar, and the solar year is the base extended period.

The length of the solar year is currently reckoned at 365.24199 days. The Gregorian calendar divides this duration into 12 uneven months — four months of 30 days, seven of 31 days and one of 28 days. On the Gregorian calendar the accrued quarter day is handled by inserting February 29th every four years. This is not necessarily the most logical or the only way of handling the accrued quarter day.

'30 days hath September, April, June and November; all the rest have 31, except for February alone, which has 28 days clear and 29 in each leap year.' So goes the folk rhyme underscoring the illogical nature of the Gregorian calendar. By contrast, a far easier and more logical way to divide the solar year would be by thirteen 28-day months with one extra free day.

The point is this: there is no logical or scientific relation between the exact length of the year and the use of the Gregorian calendar to measure and divide that length.

Nonetheless, the Gregorian calendar is held up as the most perfect instrument for dividing time, and is in use worldwide as the official standard. Although the lunation-based calendars of Islam, the Hindus, Jews and Chinese are still used for religious or ritual purposes, in daily economic and political affairs the Gregorian calendar prevails throughout the planet. How and why did this happen? What is the Gregorian calendar and where did it come from? Why do we continue to use it? Indeed what is the relationship between calendars and human behavior?

If one looks under the heading 'calendar' in the Micropaedia of the 1985 edition of *The Encyclopaedia Britannica*, a full 80% of the entry is devoted to the Gregorian calendar. This exemplifies the unquestioned authority granted to the Gregorian calendar. What is the basis of this authority?

The Gregorian calendar is dogma because no one questions it, nor wants to question it. The Gregorian calendar is the foundation of the 12:60 timing frequency.

All authority granted to this calendar is actually an allegiance to a late medieval Christian timing device. The authority of this device is held by the Vatican, geographically the smallest political state on the planet, yet given full political protection by the major Western powers (the G-7: USA, Canada, United Kingdom, France, Germany, Italy and Japan).

The irregularly numbered and irrationally named 12-month Gregorian Calendar came about as a result of a Papal Bull issued by Pope Gregory in 1572 and implemented October 5-15, 1582. The historical context in which this calendar became the fixed standard is of the greatest significance. European power, instigated by acquisitive material greed and the Church's need to gather all souls under its cross, had literally straddled the globe. Henceforth, no one could receive the 'blessings' of Christianity without receiving the Gregorian calendar.

In Europe itself, the Gregorian calendar succeeded at the precise moment when the final mechanization of time was being achieved. By AD 1600 the 12-month year and the 60-minute hour had become the established standard of time.

Thus, accompanying and giving form to the very origins of modern materialistic science was the final codification of the third-dimensional timing frequency, the 12:60. Needless to say, the authority and impact of this timing frequency was never questioned, much less realized. Though men like Kepler and Galileo were persecuted by the Church, they did not question the authority of the calendar. And so it has been with virtually all men and women of science — they accept without question this calendar by which they live.

It is to the fundamental discredit of all modern science and the society governed by its principles that it has continued to unquestioningly accept living under what is essentially a medieval yoke of time. The Gregorian calendar is a hypnotic spell which holds all the unresolvable issues of history hidden in its illogical sequence of days, weeks, months and years. Following this calendar can only lead to the place where we find ourselves today: a season of apocalypses, where disaster, ignorance and error perpetuate themselves in grinding mindlessness.

The dark apocalyptic disasters of history can only repeat themselves under this medieval yoke of time. This is how Sarajevo could be the flashpoint for World War One in AD 1914, and an unresolved battleground in AD 1995. On an even vaster scale, under this medieval yoke, we see how Babylon at the beginning of history is now the stage-set for the end of history in present-day Iraq.

Clearly, history is not democratic, and democracy itself is a hoax to keep us in the illusion of power and security. History is the script of those in power, and whoever holds the power writes the history. No one was ever asked about the Gregorian calendar, and so we all follow it as if this were the only way to deal with time.

No one has ever considered the effects of the timing frequency or standard under which we live, nor have we ever been given the opportunity to consider 'what if?' Yes, what if we lived under a different standard of time? Ask the Australian aborigine, the Amazon forest dweller, the Native American on the 'res' (reservation) what happened to their time and you will soon see that it is in the interest of the G-7 and the Vatican to keep you confused.

The Gregorian calendar is based on the original Babylonian model which substituted a measurement of space for a measurement of time. Time is not space. Time is of the mind. A circle on a flat plane divided into twelve 30° parts was used as the model for the annual calendar. A circle on a flat plane has 360° (30 x 12). One annual orbit of the Earth around the Sun is 365¼ days. The measure of time according to the standard of the circle on a flat plane is irregular, arbitrary and irrational. As is the measure of time, so is the measure of our mind.

In AD 1582, when Pope Gregory XIII cut ten days off the Julian calendar and ordained the final version of the Babylonian calendar, the mechanical clock achieved its final perfection. Using the same flat plane circle of 12, the clock doubled the 12 to 24 hours and the degrees from 30 to 60 minutes per hour.

Taxes, war and government were already secondary institutions of the human mind due to the 5,000-year use of the 12-month calendar throughout the Old World. But combined with the mechanical clock which doubled the measure, the 12:60 artificial timing frequency was locked into place as the irregular and mechanically accelerating mental condition of the human race, setting it apart from the rest of nature. Now added to taxes, war and government was the machine.

Without the mechanical clock there would be no machine, and all industrial technology would be impossible. By adjusting our biological rhythm to the accelerated 12:60 artificial time machine frequency, we humans began the acceleration of our own biological activity, with the consequent time bomb of overpopulation which plagues us today.

The tick-tock of the clock is the artificial heart ('old ticker') of Mammon. Mammon is the diabolical ghost in the machine that is living us, that is using our accelerated biological reproduction to create a total machine world. The triumph of Mammon is the triumph of materialism. The first phase of Mammon was the creation of the Babylonian 12-month government system of taxes and wages for labor. The second phase of Mammon was the clock-based machine.

Today there is no machine without money, no money without a machine, and no nation without money. Nationalism is perverted into the 12:60 dogma of war and money. But in the biosphere all boundaries are illusory.

Time and the biosphere: beyond nationalism

The 12-month Gregorian calendar has nothing to do with the annual biological rhythm of the human species in harmony with the biosphere.

A clock does not measure time. A clock measures increments of space which, projected as increments of time, are valorized into monetary units. Money does not grow on trees. Money is a function of false time.

No one owns the biosphere. No one owns time. True time does not produce money. Time is of the biosphere.

Thirteen moons, 28 days is the biosphere's measure of the

annual human biological rhythm. Twenty-eight days, 13 times a year, is the human female menstruation cycle. Everything is born of woman. To kill a woman, to harm a child, is to destroy the future. This is the 12:60 way, the way of war.

By adopting the 13-moon, 28-day calendar and rejecting the Gregorian calendar, humans will take the first step beyond the collective self-destruction bred by nationalism and the biospheric self-destruction bred by Mammon (money-machine).

More dogma to be questioned: Virtually all governments, the Vatican and banking institutions worldwide operate by the 12-month Gregorian calendar. This calendar denies and covers up the true annual human biological cycle conserved in the body of woman. Why are virtually all government leaders men? Why is it that men make war? Why is it men who run all the banks? Why are only men allowed to be priests in the Catholic Church?

Only by rejecting worldwide the 12-month Gregorian calendar and adopting immediately as the new world standard the 13-moon, 28-day calendar does the human species have any hope of resolving the suicidal deadlock of nationalism and the biosphere-destroying monetary politics which now governs the nations. Only by adopting the 13-moon calendar will endless conflicts such as the Palestinian/Israeli and Bosnian/Serbian ultimately be resolved.

Only by unifying bioregionally under the new calendar which supports all spiritual views and values equally, but does not affirm nationalism, will we find a new covenant to take us beyond war into a peace that is more than just the absence of war.

Insofar as the United Nations affirms and upholds nationalism, it is biospherically obsolete. Insofar as the United Nations affirms world peace, the United Nations' greatest peace-making operation will be to supervise the dismantling of the nation states which it now supports to the detriment of the biosphere, transforming itself thereby into the Autonomous People's Biospheric Union of the One Sovereign Earth.

This the United Nations can do by promoting, adopting and implementing the 13-moon calendar, the 13-Moon Calendar Change Peace Plan and the Pax Cultura Pax Biospherica Five-Year Plan, effective White Electric Wizard (July 26, AD 1995).

Without the 13-moon calendar change at the top of the list of peace agenda priorities, there will be no lasting peace. If the United Nations can place the 13-moon calendar change at the top of its peace agenda list, it will prove to the people of the planet that it is more than a sub-contractor of the United States State Department.

After 50 years, and more than 150 wars and 20 million war-dead, the 13-moon calendar change is the biosphere's last ultimatum to the United Nations to transcend the dogmas of nationalism and the Gregorian calendar and help bring true peace to planet Earth.

In God We Trust: Concerning the False Religion, Time is Money

The 12-month Gregorian calendar is the annual measure of the dogma 'time is money'. The mechanical clock / 60-minute hour is the daily measure of the dogma 'time is money'. Punching in and out of the time clock is the measure of the worth of our time — in money. This is the essence of 12:60 life. 12:60 is the manifest error in time which we all live, an error which is costing us the biosphere.

Money is the power ascribed to God which is worshipped and feared by all. 'In God We Trust' inscribed on the American dollar bill is the evidence of the dogma that 'time is money' and money is God's most trusted partner.

The American dollar bill is the world standard of the 12:60 dogma 'time is money'. The world's stock markets are the temples where the religion 'time is money' is propagated on a daily basis, five days a week, and its rituals of worship performed. In the stock market all human values translated into shares of competing industries are traded against an index of arbitrarily manipulated monetary units dominated by the presence of the almighty dollar.

'In God we trust, time is money' is the false religion which governs all human activity on the planet today, AD 1995, according to the pseudo-ideology of monetary politics.

In abolishing the 12-month Gregorian calendar and replacing it with the biospherically accurate 13-moon calendar, the foundation of the dogma 'time is money' is destroyed. Destroy the power of money and the power of the machine is also destroyed.

Money is the life-blood of the machine whose heart is the mechanical clock. The machine is the body of Mammon, the form of Mammon. Mammon feeds on humans. The flesh and bones of Mammon are constructed of the resources of nature. As Mammon proliferates in ever more ingenious forms, human population swells unceasingly, and the biosphere is reduced in its capacity to sustain the entropic, out-of-control excesses of the 12:60 dogma 'time is money'.

As long as the 12:60 timing frequency maintains its inert momentum, the machine can only multiply and propagate, requiring an accelerated increase in humans to devour and natural resources to waste.

Yes, to think about the Gregorian calendar is to think about the unthinkable. But if you do not take the time to start thinking about it now, you may forfeit the only time you have got.

From 13 *Moons in Motion*

FIVE

Of Moons, Mayans and the 13-Moon Calendar

Through most of its 26,000-year history, homo sapiens has followed the moon and used moon calendars. The moon is fickle and erratic. It is of nature, subtle and elusive. By current reckoning, it turns on its axis every 29.5 days, the length of a synodic lunation, which is why we always only see one side of the moon.

A synodic lunation of 29.5 days, the duration of one moon cycle seen from the Earth, is only one of the lunation cycles from which lunar compilations can be made. There is also the sidereal lunation cycle of 27.33 days (the time it takes for the moon to return to a fixed point in the sky); the 27.32 tropical cycle (taken from the celestial longitude), and the draconic cycle of 27.2 days (the time it takes the moon to return to the same node).

Right up to the 20th century pre-agricultural humans, such as the Lakota, have followed a vague or unfixed moon calendar. The fact is that during one solar year there is always a 13th lunation which transits from one solar year to the next. The taboo nature of the number 13 seems to stem from the mysterious 13th moon. There is an 11-day discrepancy between the length of the solar year of 365.242199 days and 12 complete synodic lunations of 354.36706 days. The number of days in 13 synodic lunations amounts to 383.5, a discrepancy of 18.25 days more than the solar year.

The discrepancy between days of the solar year and lunation cycles only became a problem for civilized *man*, for woman has always naturally carried the 13 moons within her being. The female menstruation cycle of 28 days is the mean between the synodic lunation cycle of 29.5 days and the other lunation cycles of less than 27.5 days. Factor the mean lunation cycle of 28 days into the solar year and the result is 13 moons, or 364 days, one day less than a mean solar year.

Once agricultural lifestyles were developed in the area of the planet now known as the Middle East, the male priesthood seized power. The question of a calendar became a matter of developing an instrument of power. The male power became associated with the sun, while the female was associated with the moon. A calendar based on the exclusivity of the solar year became paramount. The Egyptian division of the circle into 360°, subdivided into 12 parts of 30° each, provided the male priesthood of Egypt and Mesopotamia with the norm for their celestially oriented 'male solar' hierarchies. This occurred some 5,000 years ago, ca. 3000 BC.

Thus, in Babylonia and Egypt were born the 12 houses of the zodiac (and traditional Western astrology) and the 12-month calendar. Since 12 months of 30 days yield only 360 days, an extra five-day purification period was added on to complete the solar year. The chief function of the Babylonian priests of the calends was to correlate the cycles of the moon with the solar year. By 1500 BC, the system of the 360 degrees of the circle divided into 12 as an approximation of or even as a replacement for the lunation cycles spread to India and China. The 12 is based on the division of space — a circle; not time — the 13 moons.

From Babylonia and Egypt the 'solar power' of the circle of 12 spread to Greece, and thence to Rome. It was Priscius Tarquinus, early emperor of Rome (616-579 BC) who is credited with the development of the calendar from which the Gregorian is ultimately derived. The names of the Gregorian months are all Latin and come from this early Roman calendar.

By the time of the rise of the Christian Church, AD 500-1000, the Roman calendar of 12 months of uneven days in disregard of the lunation cycles was an established fact. At the beginning of the Age of Conquest, AD 1500, it was known as the Julian calendar and was based on the synodic year of 365.25 days. The Gregorian calendar is based on the tropical year of 365.242199 days.

However minute the fractional difference is between the synodic and tropic years, it should not obscure the actuality that the Gregorian calendar is an uneven and illogical distribution of days derived from a male priesthood tradition that stems from Babylonian civilization. It is a tradition of time-reckoning based on the Egyptian division of the circle, which is a division of space and not time, and in which all taboos of the number 13 are fully incorporated.

It is precisely this power of 13, associated with witchcraft and the devil, that the conquering Europeans confronted head-on when they arrived in the 'New World'. For here was a tradition of time and knowledge even more precise and fully developed than in Europe, completely based on the 13. We are referring here to the calendrical and mathematical system of the Maya upon which all Mesoamerican (Mexico and Central America) civilization was based.

There was no chance of real dialogue where the Christian priests and their zealous soldiers were concerned. People of learning were put to death, and libraries burned. The world was deprived of an understanding of time that was based not on the spatial divisions of the circle but on the lunar-galactic power of 13.

Of course, because of the hypnotic spell of the Gregorian calendar — the Dreamspell of history — you will not find a discussion on the Mayan understanding of time in the *Encyclopaedia Britannica* entry on calendars. That is the *Mayan Factor*, the overlooked factor in any accounting of human affairs. Yet if we remain only in the spell of the Gregorian calendar and ignore the Mayan Factor, then truly we are lost.

The Mayan timing frequency is 13:20 and not 12:60. Thirteen refers to the 13 galactic tones or powers of creation, which are also encoded in the 13 moons or annual lunations. Twenty refers to the 20 solar frequencies encoded as the 20 icons or solar seals. Upon this timing frequency was based the *tzolkin* or 260-kin 'sacred calendar'.

Combined with the solar cycle of 365 days, the tzolkin gave the Maya the fractal yardstick by which they could construct calendars and timing systems that demonstrate the harmonic order of the solar system and galaxy in general. Within these constructs, the Maya also maintained their lunar calendars and eclipse cycles of utmost precision.

Because the basis of the Mayan calendar was the 260-kin tzolkin and not the 360° circle, there was no need to correlate the lunation cycle to the solar year through the abstract concept of 'months'. The Mayan mathematic, based on an elegant and more sophisticated dot-bar notation system, is vigesimal not decimal — that is, based on 20s rather than 10s. This gives the Mayan mathematical system a fractal and exponential flexibility not exhibited by the decimal or duodecimal (by 12s) system upon which the Gregorian calendar is based.

Instead of months, the Mayan solar year is divided into eighteen 20-day periods called *vinals*. In actuality the 18 vinals, plus the five-day *vayeb*, were a means of correlating the solar year to the 13:20-based tzolkin.

Long a puzzle to Western archeologists, who early on understood its amazing sophistication and complexity, the Mayan calendar and mathematics have nonetheless been regarded as an anomalous curiosity, with no application to the modern world. Again, this prejudice must be seen as a function of the 12:60 consensus reality.

The fact of the matter is that the Mayan calendar contains the teaching of fourth-dimensional time that has eluded modern science, immersed as it is in the unexamined grip of third-dimensional Gregorian time. The nub of the Mayan teaching is the application of the 13:20 frequency to the creation and implementation of the calendar of the 13 moons.

From *13 Moons in Motion*

SIX

Breaking the Barrier: Releasing Ourselves from the Spell of History

To grasp the distinction between 12:60 third-dimensional time and 13:20 fourth-dimensional time is to break the barrier of the consensus reality of materialism which now dooms all of our planetary existence.

Being based on a 12-part division of space which denies the power of the 13th moon, *which is the power of time,* the Gregorian calendar consigns the consensus reality which accepts it to living exclusively in the third dimension, the plane of physical reality. In this lies the rise of the gargantuan, many-headed hydra of materialism which reduces humans to enslavement to a material technology and degrades the planetary environment without hope of any other economic lifestyle options.

To break the grip of third-dimensional time blindly and illogically incorporated in the Gregorian calendar is to break the spell of history and to release humanity once again into the natural order of reality. The accomplishment of this monumental task may be rendered heroic and celebratory by the relinquishing of the Gregorian calendar and the acceptance of the 13-moon calendar. Thirteen is the key to the Mayan galactic codes of fourth-dimensional time, *and* to the annual lunation cycles by which Earth is guided in her solar path.

The solar year, incorporating mean lunation and menstrual cycles, is most logically divided into thirteen 28-day months or moons, with one extra or free day. Auguste Comte (1798-1857, galactic signature: Red Galactic Dragon), French philosopher, founder of sociology and the school of logical positivism, first initiated the perpetual calendar of 13 months of 28 days each. The extra 365th day he termed 'year day', which was to fall between December 28 and January 1. During the 1930s a calendar reform movement utilizing the perpetual 13-month calendar gained wide official acceptance, only to be terminated by the Second World War.

The time has come again. The hour of destiny calls upon humanity to relinquish addiction to prejudice and illogical traditions of all kinds if there is to be another generation. The perpetual 13-moon calendar presents itself one more time. In this presentation, the calendar of the 13 moons is backed not only by logic but by its link to the complete codes of fourth-dimensional time, the Mayan codes, the codes of the *Dreamspell: The Journey of Timeship Earth 2013*.

In these codes are to be found the basis of movement through time, the means of social reorganization for the purpose of regenerating the Earth, and of allowing and granting forgiveness and equality to all. The call is out: Convene now in the Planetary Calendar Councils. Disseminate the knowledge of the 13 Moons in Motion. Gather and prepare for the new time.

From *13 Moons in Motion*

SEVEN

The 13-Moon Calendar: A Vehicle
of Liberation

The 13-moon calendar is a special application of the 13-tone wavespell cosmology. The wavespell is the form-in-time of universal life. Universal life means that everything is alive. Since everything takes its form in time, time is life, time is biology, galactic biology, cosmic biology. The wavespell is actually a fourth-dimensional form of life, and may assume the qualities of a living being.

As a living being, the wavespell of the 13-moon calendar is a planetary vehicle of liberation and enlightenment. The 13-moon calendar is a vehicle which has the power of automatically and simultaneously entering every human on the planet into the new time of galactic culture on Earth.

The new time of the 13 moons is the new path of life for creating equality and non-aggression on planet Earth. Once entered into, the new time of the 13-moon calendar synchronizes all humans with themselves and with the planet. Confusion will be eliminated, and forgiveness and liberation may be instantly granted. This liberation is the liberation from fear and ignorance. Why and how?

The 13-moon calendar places everyone in the correct time: now. The 13-moon calendar is without a history. It does not drag a past forward, but brings the galactic order into focus, in the now. Now is without a history. The correct time is now, and the only enlightenment is now. Any now can be as simple as a breath of air, or as complex and overlaid as a profound meditative reflection.

Now-centered and without a history, the wavespell of the 13-moon calendar is a vehicle of salvation for all of humanity and the planet.

The 13-moon calendar is a skillful means provided by the Galactic Federation to enable every human to experience her or his own enlightenment. By following the 13-moon calendar, the human enters the perfect form of the annual planetary wavespell. The wavespell is the living galactic unit of time. It is the cosmobiological indicator of higher dimensional experience. It is the way lower dimensional existence evolves and awakens into its galactically enlightened form.

As an annual planetary wavespell, the 13-moon calendar describes the galactically attuned enlightenment body of planet Earth. This is why it is a complete vehicle and path of liberation from the confusion and torment of not knowing in the now — which is enlightenment. As a description of the enlightenment body of the Earth-in-time, the calendar of the 13-moon wavespell can bring all humans into enlightenment in the course of eight solar-lunar years.

From *13 Moons in Motion*

EIGHT

To Become a Planetary Kin, Follow the 13 Moons

To enter the 13-moon path is to enter a new world of time, a world of wavespells, pulsars and overtone pulsars, of harmonics, chromatics and galactic spins. The 13-moon calendar is the day-by-day approach to learning and living the different holon simultaneities of the fourth dimension. By following the path of the calendar of the 13 moons, every human has the opportunity of becoming a planetary kin.

A planetary kin is a galactic enzyme passing through the wavespell-body of Earth-in-time. Because the 13-moon calendar is perfectly attuned to and coded by the 260-kin galactic spin, by following the path of the 13 moons, any human is also imprinted by the 260 kin of the galactic spin. These 260 kin are the galactic enzyme codes of interdimensional existence. Understanding the interdimensional nature of existence, a planetary kin, free and equal with all other planetary kin, furthers the forces of galactic evolution and universal enlightenment.

Correct understanding of the fourth dimension enables the planetary kin to understand the ignorance of deathfear, the chief failure of third-dimensional will. Overcoming deathfear, the planetary kin can dissolve the mental paralysis caused by belief in technology as a solution, and release him- or herself from civilization understood as material infrastructure to be maintained at all costs. The only intelligent choice remaining to a planetary kin is the pursuit of universal life: telepathy and higher collective bonding with all of existence.

This transformative process is rendered natural and ordinary by the planetary service wavespell, the easy way of learning how to walk the path of the 13-moon calendar and to gain full entry into the fourth dimension.

From *13 Moons in Motion*

NINE

Arcturian Almanac: Dreamspell Catalog of Mayan Cycles

Historical note

Dreamspell: the Journey of Timeship Earth 2013 is a pure formulation and updating of the mathematical calendar codes originally brought to this planet by the Maya. The Dreamspell is a new dispensation of time for our time. No one knew better than the Maya, nor recorded more accurately, the precise nature of the many cycles of time in which the Earth is involved as a planetary body within a galactic star system.

It was the intention of the Maya that their formulation of time, based on a frequency code of 13:20 (13 galactic tones, 20 solar frequencies), was to be a gift contributing to the fulfillment of human consciousness on planet Earth. Like the Hopi awaiting the Pahana, 'the lost white brother', the Maya awaited the arrival of their kin from the far side of the Atlantic.

On October 12, AD 1492 (Dreamspell 7 Earth of the year 7 Storm), Christopher Columbus arrived in the 'New World'. The hopes of the Maya, the Hopi and all indigenous people, not only of the Americas but of the entire planet, were thoroughly shattered and destroyed. Genocide, enslavement and colonization were the indigenous people's reward. Never had the knowledge of a high civilization been so intentionally desecrated and destroyed as was that of the Maya.

In one single act of conquest, humanity was deprived of the gift of the knowledge of time. By 1583 the Catholic Church installed its 'reform' of time known as the Gregorian calendar. Simultaneous to the proclamation of the Gregorian calendar was the development of mechanized time, the basis of all machine technology. Instead of the 13:20 galactic frequency of time, the planet was bequeathed the 12:60 (12-month year, 60-minute hour) frequency of machine technology.

The 12:60 frequency of machine technology is surrogate time, which in actuality is based on standards of measurement of space. In the scientific and industrial revolutions that followed, the dominating, materialistic and acquisitive Western mind engulfed the planet.

This same mind now seeks to conquer space as well. Humanity today is driven and obsessed by a space-based science and mathematics. In solely recognizing space without understanding time, science has created a crippled, suicidal race of enslaved humans helplessly living in a rapidly deteriorating planetary environment.

Until the human race is willing to own its mistake of living in the wrong time and removing itself from the influence of this wrong time, humanity has no hope whatsoever of curing itself of the problems which it alone has created.

The most immediate first step that needs to be taken is to relinquish the Gregorian calendar, replacing it instead with the mathematically accurate calendar of the 13 moons. The 13-moon calendar, *13 Moons in Motion,* is the cornerstone of the new Mayan dispensation of time, *Dreamspell: the Journey of Timeship Earth 2013.* The Dreamspell is an information revolution for all of humanity that is based on the mathematics of time. Where space is the third dimension, time is the fourth dimension.

The mathematics of time has nothing to do with the mathematics of space. The mathematics of time is based on whole numbers and fractals; it is radial and not linear. This fourth-dimensional mathematic consists of interlocking sets of cycles that repeat with different significances through ever more expanding levels.

It is of the utmost importance that the knowledge of time as the *13 Moons in Motion* be disseminated through all media and education systems of the planet as rapidly as possible, and that the Gregorian calendar be relinquished as soon as possible. Once humanity is operating on the correct standard of time, it will have a proper basis of unification for accomplishing the enormous and heroic task that now challenges it.

Greater than any spiritual teaching is the gift of time.

Note: Dreamspell years are not the same as classic Mayan reckoning. As a new dispensation of galactic time, Dreamspell takes its count from -23,987 (BC). All discrepancy of time and leap year days are assumed and accounted for in this reckoning. It is commonly agreed that the Mayan Great Cycle has as its point of departure the approximate date of August 13, 3113 BC. In Dreamspell years this date is -3187. The discrepancy of 74 years is absorbed in the Dreamspell as a function of the new dispensation of time.

Like the 13-moon calendar, the Dreamspell has no history. It is an overlay of galactic time intended to help humans overcome their disturbed and conflicting views of history. The common point between the Mayan tradition as it survived and the Dreamspell is the galactic synchronization Gregorian calendar date July 26 (July 16, Julian or pre-Gregorian calendar), which always falls on one of the four gateway solar seals: Red Moon, White Wizard, Blue Storm, Yellow Seed.

The Dreamspell is truly galactic in origin. Its comprehensive set of cyclic fractals is like a set of lenses that view the Earth and its solar system from the fourth dimension. It is neither heliocentric nor geocentric, but both and beyond. More than science or theory, the Dreamspell is meant to be lived. The key into the Dreamspell for the mass of humanity at this time is the calendar *13 Moons in Motion*.

According to the Dreamspell, Columbus arrived in America during a 7 Storm year. This 7 Storm year occurs 520 later in the year AD 2012. The celebration of the 500th anniversary of Columbus's arrival occurred in a 13 Storm year, AD 1992. This celebration was actually the announcement of the final katun of the 5200-year, 260-katun Great Cycle of the Maya and of the 26,000-year, 1300-katun planetary Dreamspell cycle.

One katun fractals all katuns. Within one scale a katun may be a day; within another scale a katun may be 1300 years or more. Though it may appear to be a superhuman effort, everything that has gone astray as a result of not understanding the Mayan gift of time can now be rectified within this final katun.

From *13 Moons in Motion*

TEN

A Short History of the 13-Moon Calendar Change Peace Movement

The 13-Moon Calendar Change Peace Movement is a galactic strategy that has its roots in the Harmonic Convergence World Peace Meditation, August 16-17 1987. The Harmonic Convergence was a prophetic release of Mayan time science. The earth exists as a planetary body within the star system Kinich Ahau, located within the experimental zone. The experiment is free will, the object of the experiment is the human species. Prophecy occurs as a corrective antidote to free will abuse within the galactic experimental zone.

The Harmonic Convergence was the fulfillment of the ancient Mexican prophecy of the 13 Heavens of decreasing choice and the Nine Hells of increasing doom. As a Mayan time release, this prophecy ran a course of 1,144 years from AD 843 to 1987. In essence this prophecy stated that if 144,000 humans could gather at sacred sites worldwide at the appointed hour, August 16-17 1987, human civilization would move into a new era of universal peace.

In actuality, the event marked the opening of the gate to the final 25 years of the Mayan Great Cycle of 13 Baktuns, BC 3113-AD 2012. The prophecy of Harmonic Convergence also made it clear that universal peace would occur, but only on the condition that humanity abandon the technological civilization of materialism and return to living in harmony with nature. If not, global catastrophe would certainly occur before the 2012, 13-Baktun closeout date.

The question for the program agents chosen for this project was the following: How were we to understand this return to nature and how would it come about?

For the purpose of understanding the nature of this project, we submitted to living completely in the timing cycles which had so accurately confirmed the dates of the Harmonic Convergence Prophecy. By living these cycles faithfully while applying research methods to their mathematical analysis of the calendar, we were liberated from a conventional materialist lifestyle.

As a consequence, in December 1989 we made the discovery of

the 12:60—13:20 timing frequencies. According to this discovery a single timing frequency governs the order of the galaxy right down to its atomic structure. This timing frequency is the fourth-dimensional order of reality, and on this planet was known only by the ancient Maya. This unifying timing frequency is the 13:20: thirteen galactic tones and 20 solar frequencies, codified as the *tzolkin* or sacred calendar round of 260 days.

The 12:60 is the false, artificial timing frequency followed solely by the human species. Twelve refers to the 12-month Gregorian/Babylonian calendar and 60 refers to the 60-minute hour of the mechanical clock. Both the 12-month calendar and the mechanical clock have their origin in the Babylonian substitution of the 12-part division of a circle in space for measurements of fourth-dimensional cycles of time. This error was institutionalized into the fabric of human civilization. As a result, the human race is today living an error in time. This error is to the detriment of its own life-support system and its future survival.

This discovery provided us with the answer to the question of how humanity was to return to nature and how this would be brought about. If the error in time was locked into the Gregorian/Babylonian calendar, then the first step leading humanity back to nature would be to replace this erroneous calendar with a calendar conforming to the correct 13:20 timing frequency. Thus was born the galactic strategy of the 13-Moon Calendar Change Peace Movement.

According to this strategy, the replacement of the 12-month Gregorian calendar by the biologically accurate 13-moon, 28-day calendar by July 26, 1992, would fulfill the requirements of the Mayan timing cycles and assure that humanity would complete its final 20-year cycle of history by living in phase once again with nature.

Telektonon tour of planetary duty: program goals and assessment

So immersed was humanity in the 12:60 timing frequency that it could not properly heed the call of the Time Shift, July 26 1992, Blue Cosmic Storm. We had decoded the mathematics of fourth-dimensional time which support and give form to the 13-moon calendar and presented these codes in their entirety as the Dreamspell tool-kit. However, the human mind had become further entrenched in its own error, and as a result could not comprehend the meaning and significance of the Dreamspell.

For this reason, July 26 1993, Yellow Magnetic Seed, Kin 144 marked the entrance to the next prophetic cycle, Telektonon. The purpose of the Telektonon is to assist in correcting the free will abuse that prevented humanity from making a collective choice that would better its own planetary course.

Telektonon, Earth Spirit Speaking Tube, is the prophecy of Pacal Votan, AD 631-683. His spectacular tomb in Palenque, Chiapas, Mexico, was sealed in AD 692 and opened in AD 1952. Telektonon refers to the oracular tube whose purposive placement leads from the tomb, up the stairway, to a temple floor atop the pyramid of the inscriptions. Had it not been for this tube, the tomb of Pacal Votan would never have been discovered.

According to this prophecy, the last seven years of the millennium, 1993-2000, constitute the end of false time, the time of judgement or the apocalypse. During this time humanity has but one decision to make if it wishes to save itself and avoid total destruction: reject the false 12-month calendar and accept in its place the 13-moon calendar. "Telektonon is revealed to you, God's plan for peace on Earth, the last and only hope for spiritual renewal and salvation: immediate acceptance and adoption of the 28-day, 13-moon way, the Calendar Telektonon."

To fulfill the prophecy, we were given a two-year planetary Telektonon tour of duty. The purpose of this tour of duty was to spread the prophecy and need of the 13-moon calendar change; to examine the conditions rendered by the 12:60 in diverse environments; to identify sites for the establishment of the galactic cultural project; and to oversee the demise of the G-7.

By July 26 1994, Red Lunar Moon, the Telektonon tour of duty had produced the 13-Moon Calendar Change Peace Movement and Peace Plan. The 13-Moon Calendar Change Peace Plan has been submitted to the United Nations, UNESCO, numerous Heads of State, Pope John Paul II, and many grass roots groups and organizations. This Peace Plan includes the 'Pax Cultura Pax Biospherica' proposal for a First World Peace, 1995-2000.

As of July 26 1995, Third Year of Prophecy, White Electric Wizard, the initial program goal of changing calendars had attained signal victory. As a result, the 13-Moon Calendar Change Peace Plan is being amended and incorporated into the Granting of Biospheric Amnesty. Bases for the establishment of the galactic cultural project have been established in Mexico, South America, North America, Western Europe and Japan.

In addition, network resources Operation Victory USA and Operation Victory Europe are in the process of extending the new calendar and related information worldwide. Finally, as will appear later in this report, a distinct cultural bioregion, the archipelago of Japan, has been selected as the pilot model for full scale social conversion into the new time.

From *'Japan' Document, September 1995*

ELEVEN
Pax Biospherica

Premise: The biosphere is governed by the principle of interdependent unity. Each and all of its constituent elements is governed and characterized by this same principle. Thus, there is only one ocean, one atmosphere, one Earth, one water, indivisible. Likewise, the DNA of life is one whole and the biodiversity of the one life exists by the same principle of interdependent unity.

The two most fundamental bases of the biosphere's cosmic existence, time and space, are also each a coherent interdependent unity. The human species, intrinsically governed by the same principle of interdependent unity, is the only exception to this law of unity.

Only the human species, by its beliefs, insists on dividing the Earth by fictitious boundaries, and is then willing to wage globally devastating wars in their defense. Only humans divide their beliefs into religious sects, and kill others for not sharing the same sectarianism. And, most fundamentally, only humans live in a time apart from the rest of the biosphere.

Only humans live by a ruthlessly accelerating mechanization of time which in turn dominates them and the planet with the production and creation of machines which increase daily along with the human population. This dual exponential acceleration of machine and human population depletes the planet's vital resources and diminishes its biodiversity at an alarming rate, threatening the interdependent fabric of the biosphere itself with an unprecedented biogeochemical transformation of toxic waste. This process, induced and maintained by living in false 12:60 time, must now be considered an unethical and immoral indulgence exceeding all proportion in violation of the biosphere's one inviolable law: interdependent unity.

Humans alone created the present situation of biospheric chaos and destruction. Humans alone can put an end to this situation by collective use of their free will synchronized in time. The first step to calling a halt to this path of self-destruction is to place ourselves back in the natural timing frequency by which the rest of the biosphere lives and is governed. This is the purpose of the 13-Moon Calendar Change Peace Movement. To change calendars is to STOP in our course and make a fundamental change in our annual timing frequency, from an irregular, unnatural frequency of 12 months to a regular, harmonic, biological frequency of thirteen 28-day moons.

This fundamental change in our timing frequency is the opportunity for establishing a new covenant based on the biosphere's principle of interdependent unity. In this way humanity may extricate itself from its slavish, self-defensive entrapment in an institutional order enmeshed in the old calendar and the old time.

We have to establish our biospheric rights in accord with the principle of interdependent unity, using the new calendar to work out a pragmatic schedule for the rapid transformation of human society, assuring its realignment within the cosmic order of the biosphere. In defining the biospheric rights of each human, the issue of money, so inextricably a part of the mechanization of time now governing humanity, must be confronted. The system of money continues to create an ever-widening inequality within the species and is now the principle tool of a merciless politics which serves to maintain the species in the deadening materialism of a global corporate monoculture.

Free ocean. Free air. Free water. Free life. Free land. These are the rights enjoyed by all other species who exist by a mutual pressure of interdependent cycles which they exert one upon another. These, in principle, are the same rights which each human individual should possess by right of birth.

Ongoing implementation of biospheric rights will be the responsibility of the coordinated groups operating bioregionally under the Banner of Peace known as the 13-Moon Calendar Change Peace Movement, Operation Victory North America, Operation Victory Europe, VictoryNet Japan, and all coordinating groups of the World Parliament of Ecumenical Unity, *Rinri* Institute and so on.

Waging the five-year Pax Biospherica

Just as World War II took five years to change the world completely, so a five-year Pax Biospherica is needed to mobilize humanity to clean up the industrial age mess, reorganize itself according to the 13:20 laws of natural time, and discover the telepathic technologies for dealing with its 12:60 problems created by materialism. If you do not think we have to do something immediately, consider this:

Every day that dawns, the planetary moment is more unprecedented than ever. How? Every day there are a quarter-million more humans, 200 less species and 61 million automobiles driving back and forth to 'work' with only one occupant, enough to circle the planet seven times, spewing untold volumes of carbon monoxide into the atmosphere already saturated with contamination. In virtually every home, including the lowest, meanest hovels of the 'ring cities' that surround every burgeoning metropolis in Latin America, Asia and Africa, there is a television set emanating daily thousands of disconnected images, selling countless products, presenting meaningless segments of game shows and Hollywood-made movies, punctuated by news broadcasts featuring the same glib, authoritarian-voiced, plastic-perfect newscasters. In thousands of high-rise apartments everywhere, bags of plastic trash bearing 'Save the Earth' slogans are dropped endlessly down thousands of garbage chutes whose terminal point is beyond the awareness of all but a few.

This is just a minute slice of life on planet Earth, Gregorian calendar AD 1995. To it we could add images of tens of thousands of cars pouring off production lines in Japan, Germany and a dozen other highly industrialized countries, the millions of barrels of oil still being pumped out of the Persian Gulf, the Gulf of Mexico, Lake Maracaibo, Saudi Arabia and Tashkent, former USSR; the underground nuclear bomb testing in the Chinese-controlled Gobi Desert and in the French-controlled area of the Pacific; and the hundreds of new shopping centers now being built on the outskirts of every global urban center.

While all of this expenditure of energy and Earth's resources is occurring in only one day, the political leadership of the planet, representing far less than one percent of the total population, is wrangling, wheeling and dealing for more trade agreements, better tariffs, more advantageous tax credits, and mutually beneficial monetary alliances to boost industrial production at home and

develop new markets in 'developing countries', or conversely beg-
ging for investments that will increase employment and bring the
'benefits' of the First World to the starving Third World. The Cold
War over, the remaining 'superpower', the United States of America, bastion of democracy, still maintains a military budget of 200
billion dollars a year.

This is the grinding daily background to our call for a Pax Biospherica, for all of this incessant and mindless human activity is at
the expense of the biosphere.

The biosphere is the living envelope of life that is being dimin-
ished, depleted and destroyed species-by-species every day that the
juggernaut of human industrial civilization continues unabated.

While most humans may not have a clue that they are a part of
the biosphere, the fact is that knowledge of the biosphere represents a notable advance in human consciousness. Care of the biosphere represents an advance in human understanding and com-
passion as well. What is happening to the biosphere and ourselves
at this very moment is actually a transition in our own evolution
and the evolution of life on Earth. Technically, this is the biogeochemical transition of the biosphere into the noosphere. Biogeochemical refers to the sum of the energy processes of life, the Sun
and the Earth, now impacted upon and augmented by the creation
of the artificial technology of human civilization. The noosphere
refers to the mental envelope represented by the conscious advance
of humanity into its next, post-technological evolutionary stage.

According to V.I. Vernadsky who first discovered and stated the
laws and principles of the biosphere in 1926 (the human population then was less than two billion; it is now approaching six billion), this moment in our evolution is characterized by

*". . . that immense new form of biogeochemical which is represented
in the biosphere by the technological work of man, complexly guided
by his thought. It is interesting that the increase, in the course of time,
of machinery in the structure of human society also proceeds in geometrical progression, just like the production of living matter, man
included ... Statesmen should be aware of the present elemental process
of transition of the biosphere into the noosphere. The fundamental prop-
erty of biogeochemical energy is clearly revealed in the growth of free*

energy in the biosphere with the progress of geological time, especial-
ly in relation to its transition into the noosphere."

(Problems in Biogeochemistry II, 1944)

Fifty years have passed since Vernadsky wrote this precise, objective statement concerning our evolutionary moment. We doubt that even a few, if any, politicians or statesmen alive today are aware of the fact that we are in a condition of transition from the biosphere to the noosphere. This transition is not a political decision, but an evolutionary shift. For this reason the evolutionary tools for making this transition, the 13-Moon Calendar, the Dreamspell and the Telektonon, are now available for all of humanity. The analysis of the 12:60—13:20 timing frequency demands that humanity rise to the occasion and begin to consciously and positively redirect its own course. The first step was the 13-Moon Calendar Change Peace Plan, July 25-26 1995. The second step is the immediate and consequent implementation of the Pax Cultura Pax Biospherica, 1995-2000.

It is Pax Cultura because peace is culture and the advancement of culture, not war and the militarily enforced absence of war. It is Pax Biospherica because, as it is now constituted, human industrial civilization is war against the biosphere which supports it. If we are to avoid imminent self-destruction, human civilization must now be immediately redirected according to the correct 13:20 timing frequency to establish itself on a post-technological basis in a renewed condition of harmony and peace with its biosphere.

Pax Biospherica: the ideology of unification

If history is defined as the play of dialectical opposites, then history ended with the tearing down of the Berlin Wall, December 31, AD 1989.

What dawned on January 1, AD 1990 was the first day of post-history.

Five years of post-history have now passed, one half of the decade of the 1990s is now over. Has the world become a better, safer place? Are human values improving? Is the environment, our biosphere, in a healthier condition? We must answer 'no' to all of these questions.

The fact of the matter is that the first five years of post-history were a spiral downward into planetary moral anarchy dominated by the monetary politics of the G-7 and the relentless onslaught of materialism. If this entropic drift is allowed to continue, it will bring the rapid end of the biosphere and the human race.

In the post-historic, post-dialectic vacuum, the Pax Biospherica is the ideology of unification needed to transcend the moral anarchy of the first post-historical stage following the end of the Cold War, AD 1990-1995.

The 13-Moon Calendar Change Peace Plan, July 24-26, AD 1995, was the dramatic, planet-unifying event to redeem the hope that flared when the Berlin Wall went down. If humanity misses the opportunity offered by the 13-Moon Calendar Change, then it will forfeit all future hope. Remember: we are the biosphere, the biosphere is greater than us. Thirteen moons is the measure of our peace with the biosphere and with ourselves.

12:60, the manifest error in time, is war against the biosphere. Because it places humans out of phase with nature, the 12:60 timing frequency relentlessly and destructively uses nature's resources against itself, provoking a state of war.

In this war, the life support system of the biosphere is reduced daily by the loss of literally hundreds of species, the increasing contamination of all vital systems, and the rupture of a delicate balance of organic and inorganic cycles. In this war, who will defend the biosphere? The Army of the Righteous will defend the biosphere.

From *13-Moon Calendar Change Peace Plan*

TWELVE

Sacred Warriors: Planet Art Network and Planetary Calendar Councils

The oracle of the third year of prophecy is signified by the return of the 'sacred warrior'. Who is the sacred warrior and what is the task that the warrior makes sacred?

The sacred warrior is one thoroughly without aggression who works creatively on behalf of the benefit of all beings for seven generations to come. Without allegiance to any chauvinism, understanding that all of life is sacred, for this moment in the cosmic cycle of evolution, the sacred warrior attunes him- or herself to the correct rhythms of time and nature in order to co-creatively and cooperatively assist in the emergence of humanity from the cocoon of 12:60 industrial entropy. This sacred task, at one with the unifying divine purpose and universal plan, is referred to as PAN — all, the whole, the unity, encompassed by the emergent form of a Planet Art Network.

The time has come to unify the arts and proclaim art as the goal and order of human society. This is consistent with the 13:20 'time is art'. Art is the only non-aggressive means to resolve the problems created by the technology of the machine and the attendant 12:60 materialism which have brought about the violent anarchic degradation of values and approaching destruction of the biosphere. It is all a matter of a simple shift in priorities in accord with the shift into the new time. 'Art now, war no more!' But art must unify and be unified, not for profit or personal gain, but for the end of realizing humanity as a planetary whole.

PAN is rooted in the principle of Dharma Art. 'Dharma' means universal norm, while art is the uninhibited practice of expressing this universal norm down to the very least detail of everyday life. 'Life as we live it is the ritual we are looking for' is a key slogan for practicing Dharma Art.

Dharma Art also recognizes the natural order or hierarchy of Heaven above, Earth below, and human in between, joining Heaven and Earth. This threefold ordering principle is explicit or implicit in all the infinite manifestations of Dharma Art. As the expression of the universal norm, which may be identified with the 13:20 timing frequency, Dharma Art is inherently sacred without being identified with any particular belief, yet inclusive of all.

As the means for establishing peace and the return of sacred order, Dharma Art is the foundation for global peace. Extended in principle and as a call to action to artists worldwide, Dharma Art becomes the Planet Art Network. In essence, the call to action declares that the time has come for the artists, not the generals and bankers, to decide the direction and to create the shape of the future of human society. The PAN vision is based on the unification of the Earth and humanity synchronized in time through new forms of ritually coordinated, telepathic exercises of artistic creation.

The Harmonic Convergence world peace meditation was an early example of this type of Planet Art Network project. In order to affirm its life-furthering mission, PAN is inseparably allied to the Pax Cultura vision of the Banner of Peace. Pax Cultura Peace Through Culture was the world peace movement of the 1930s whose major achievement was the creation of the Roerich Peace Pact (1935).

This peace pact, which officially called for the flying of the Banner of Peace over all artistic, scientific, educational and cultural monuments and institutions in times of war, is still recognized by international law as a valid instrument of peace. One of the purposes of PAN is to fully reawaken this instrument of peace on behalf of the new time of biospheric rights.

Planet Art Network and the Planetary Calendar Councils

Though five years have passed since the end of the Cold War, the unilateral grip of the G-7 and the shadow of nuclear politics and disasters still dominate the planetary theater of events. 'Wars and rumors of wars', terrorism and mind manipulations of insidious kinds and degrees make the need for a Planet Art Network stronger than ever before.

The eight years of Harmonic Convergence marked by the signal victory of the 13-Moon Calendar Change Peace Movement, inaugurating the third year of prophecy, have sounded the new call for the Planet Art Network. Unprecedented network unification and coordination have roused Operation Victory USA and Operation Victory Europe to join the ranks of the autonomous, self-organizing Latin American 13-Moon Calendar Change peace groups. Operation Victory Japan is now being formed.

Entrance into the new time of 13 moons and ultimately into the fourth-dimensional operating reality of the new time necessitates yet another level of group coordination: Planetary Calendar Councils and the Planet Art Network. In principle the PCCs and PAN are two wings of the new bird of true time. The PCCs are responsible for 13:20 program content and education, while PAN is responsible for pattern and form of implementation.

It must be understood that gradually over the next three to five years all current social forms will be subordinated to and transformed by the cyclic orders of the new time. Greatly assisting the process of the 13-Moon Calendar harmonization of the human realm will be *Telektonon*, game of prophecy and technology of telepathy, and the *Dreamspell* tool kit for navigating fourth-dimensional time. These three instruments form three levels of the galactic knowledge of time, the basis of galactic culture:

1) The *13-Moon Calendar* constitutes galactic kindergarten where humans may actually learn and experience the difference between the false time of the 12:60 (12-month calendar) and the true time of the 13:20.

2) *Telektonon, Game of Prophecy*, introduces the universal daily chronometer of 13 moons/28 days and the initial principles of the technology of telepathy. Use and practice of the *Telektonon* constitutes galactic primary and secondary school.

3) *Dreamspell, the Journey of Timeship Earth 2013*, consisting of the complete proofs and operating tools for navigating fourth-dimensional time, provides the complete curriculum for the galactic university.

Overseeing the production of these three educational tools will be the responsibility of the various Operation Victory networks of the 13-Moon Calendar Change Peace Movement working on a bioregional basis. While major private and corporate sponsorship and distribution according to the principle of the 'potlatch' is the desired goal, in the interim a simple, direct marketing approach is to be followed where all profit will be used to support the network operations and living expenses of teachers.

One of the chief functions of the Planetary Calendar Councils will be to coordinate the purchase and distribution of calendars, games and kits from the bioregional Operation Victory network, and thence to coordinate the teachers, markets and teaching programs. Working with other light groups and positive social action organizations, the goal of the PCCs will be to interface with the existing 12:60 social forms to initiate the process of transformation.

Planet Art Network is the unification of artists worldwide for coordination and synchronization of planet art events, fostering experimentation and implementation of the new 13:20 social forms articulated by the PCCs. PCCs and PAN are mutually self-organizing, autonomous and self-evolving. PCCs operate locally, while PAN implements globally. The local PCCs may develop a schedule of meetings or round-tables in accord with the annual Planetary Service Wavespell. Through the Operation Victory networks, the PCCs will be in contact with each other worldwide for coordination of learning programs and sponsorship of periodic symposia, conferences, etc., to integrate the new knowledge.

The PCCs are the spiritual 13-Moon Victory Base grounding nodes for the recovery of the sacred. Operating from these bases, the PAN provides the spiritual 13-Moon Victory Sacred Warrior program implementation.

PAN: the ten-year program

Because it is in accord with the 13:20 cycles and timing frequency, PAN is cosmically ordained. The 13-Moon PAN Victory March, 1995-2005, is the biospheric protection and renewal plan, the answer to the G-7. PAN extends the 13-Moon Peace Plan forward from the completion of biospheric amnesty, Crystal Moon 28, '13-Moon Victory Day', third year of prophecy. The forthcoming 52 days of victory and PAN's First Olympics of Cooperation is just the beginning of the complete ten-year program of planetary transformation.

The PAN ten-year program is inclusive of the five years of the First World Peace 1995-2000 and the first five years of Heaven on Earth, 2000-2005. Occurring within the context of the Harmonic

Operation Victory USA/Europe, Planetary Calendar Councils and Planet Art Network coordinate to interface with existing 12:60 social forms to initiate processes of social transformation

NEW 13:20 TRANSFORMATIONAL SOCIAL STRUCTURES

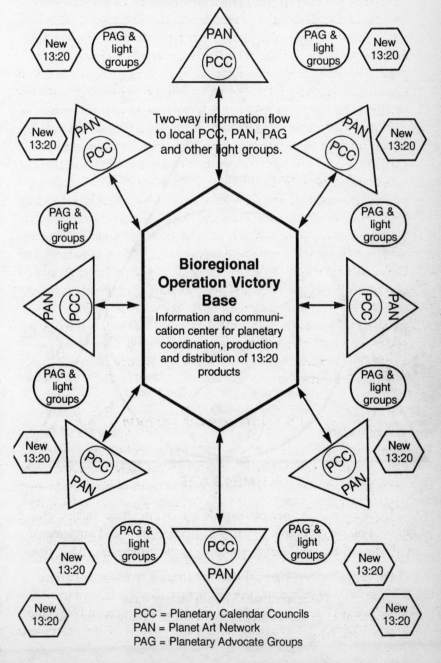

Two-way information flow to local PCC, PAN, PAG and other light groups.

Bioregional Operation Victory Base
Information and communication center for planetary coordination, production and distribution of 13:20 products

PCC = Planetary Calendar Councils
PAN = Planet Art Network
PAG = Planetary Advocate Groups

TIME IS ART
PCC-PAN
Organizational Model

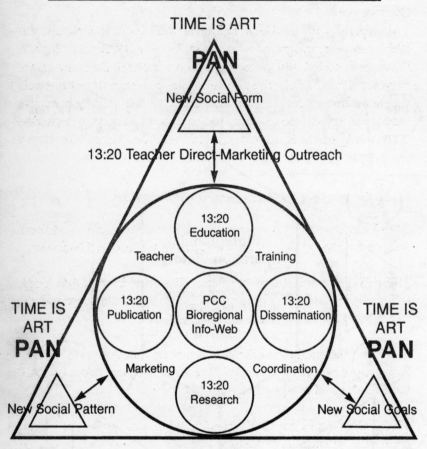

PAN: Unification of Artists planetwide for coordination and synchronization of planet art events fostering experimentation and implementation of new artistic social forms according to the principles of 13:20 time.

Self-organizing — Autonomous — Self-evolving

PCC: Spiritual 13-Moon Victory Base
PAN: Spiritual 13-Moon Victory Sacred Warrior Program Implentation

Convergence prophecy, the PAN ten-year program occupies the critical run from the overtone tower of the last 13 years of history through the overtone tower of the first 13 years of Heaven on Earth (see *Dreamspell* 'Galactic Compass, Timeship Earth 2013, 26-Year Countdown').

In accord with the Galactic Federation's cultural strategy, the PAN ten-year program is defined by the Planetary Service Wavespells coded into the names and functions of the solar-galactic years, 1995-2005. In the five last years of history the wavespell functions are in reverse. At the point of the millennium, the wavespell spins into its fourth-dimensional, counter-clockwise direction. Remember, all solar-galactic years begin July 26 and end the following July 25, Gregorian dates.

I. Last five years of the last 13-year wavespell of history

1995-1996: Overtone Command Tower, White Electric Wizard, third year of prophecy, 'Victory Pacifies', activate Planet Art Network.

1996-1997: Third Self-Existing Form Chamber, Blue Self-Existing Storm, fourth year of prophecy, 'Victory Establishes', define 13-Moon PAN social order and biospheric goals.

1997-1998: Second Electric Service Chamber, Yellow Overtone Seed, fifth year of prophecy, 'Victory Releases', command 13-Moon PAN social order and biospheric tasks.

1998-1999: First Lunar Challenge Chamber, Red Rhythmic Moon, sixth year of prophecy, 'Victory Purifies', administer equality of artistic activity for all in the purification of the biosphere.

1999-2000: Magnetic Gate of Purpose, White Resonant Wizard, seventh year of prophecy, 'Victory Discharges', attune to Earth for great art of time shift completion: biosphere-noosphere transition.

II. First five years of 13-year Heaven on Earth

2000-2001: Magnetic Gate of Purpose, Blue Galactic Storm, first year of Heaven on Earth, PAN establishes Earth as a galactic evolutionary model of unified consciousness.

2001-2002: First Lunar Challenge Chamber, Yellow Solar Seed, second year of Heaven on Earth, PAN pulses intention of realizing solar consciousness as biotelepathic norm.

2002-2003: Second Electric Service Chamber, Red Planetary Moon, third year of Heaven on Earth, PAN manifests planetary order through service of social form on behalf of fulfillment of solar consciousness.

2003-2004: Third Self-Existing Form Chamber, White Spectral Wizard, fourth year of Heaven on Earth, PAN attains social wisdom of dissolving all previous means of attainment for release into solar consciousness.

2004-2005: Overtone Command Tower, Blue Crystal Storm, fifth year of Heaven on Earth, PAN attains universal cooperation of galactic memory at the planetary round table in order to catalyze forthcoming entry into the Green Central Castle of the Galactic Federation.

Note: solar consciousness refers to the fourth-dimensional telepathic order for stabilizing the genetic coding of the species at a new level of environmental harmonization.

PAN: Time is art, definition of new social forms and goals according to Telektonon-Dreamspell

Over the remaining five years of prophecy, PAN will emerge as the nervous system of the new telepathic order of human society. Gradually, all social forms will be subordinated to and transformed by the form and order of the new time of 13 moons. Within three years money will cease to be a social organizing principle and instrument for the accumulation of artificial wealth. As this occurs, true time will emerge as the supreme ordering principle and all present forms of social interaction will attain increasingly artistic levels of sophistication.

Inherent in the 13-Moon Calendar, the Telektonon and Dream-spell are the new forms of social organization and behavior. The 13-Moon Calendar reorganizes the human biological frequency according to its natural annual rhythm. The effect is at first subtle, but after one year establishes an inner harmony and after two years induces a telepathic field. These effects are both restorative, offset-ting the lifestyle of the machine, and cumulative in proportion to the collective numbers following the new calendar of 13 moons.

The general biotelepathic field of resonance created by an increasing mass of humanity following the 13-Moon Calendar is augmented by the Telektonon. By following the Telektonon Jour-ney inclusive of the 16-day Warrior's Labyrinth through its full 28-day cycle moon after moon, the human biotelepathic circuit attains increasing conscious articulation and effectiveness.

The Telektonon playing board and daily chronometer are the nuts and bolts of the new developing technology of telepathy. Inher-ent within the Telektonon are layerings of time cycles which pen-etrate the unconscious and subliminal conscious fields of the mind. The sum of the effects of the Telektonon are described by the title of one of the subsets of its 52 cards: 'The Telepathic Redemption of the Lost Planets'.

While the 13-Moon Calendar and the Telektonon fulfill the pur-pose of biologically and telepathically restoring the human to its rightful role and place within the planetary biosphere, it is the Dreamspell which provides the social reorganizing factor of the new time. Integrated within the matrix of the 13-moon Telektonon, the Dreamspell play fulfills to the maximum the premise 'time is art'.

The Dreamspell offers the full complement of the interactive orders of 13:20 time. While the 13-Moon Calendar and the Telek-tonon are necessary for the transition from the third-dimensional error in time to the fourth-dimensional supremacy of time and telepathy, the Dreamspell establishes the actual artistic workings of humanity evolving toward its planetary fulfillment.

One of the principle functions of the Planetary Calendar Coun-cils will be to educate for action concerning the different 13:20 tim-ing cycles. It is the purpose of the Planet Art Network to coordinate and synergize the increasing numbers of humans operating by these 13:20 cycles into greater and ever more unified acts of planetary art.

While it will be the task of the local PCCs to explore the manner in which the new cycles may be used to convert thought and energy of the old time into the purposive order of the new time, these cycles may be summarized as follows:

I. Biotelepathic Cycle (364+1 days)

28-day cycle: normative biotelepathic rhythm, 13 per year, for re-establishing biospheric normalcy of the human species.

7-day week: base unit for transiting from third-dimensional order of time to fourth-dimensional telepathy; four 7-day weeks, each endowed with a prophetic power of cosmic form, constitute 28-day Telektonon cycle, 52 weeks per year.

16-day Warrior's Labyrinth Journey (days 7-22 of every 28-day Moon): this is the intensified span of time for collective telepathic unification of mind, spirit and will for the purpose of restoring the Law of the Cube, the original divine plan and order of reality.

13-Moon Planetary Service Wavespell: annual restorative biotelepathic cycle collectively organized for planetary service, each with a specific goal toward realizing the prophetic closing of the millennium and the transformation of human society from biospheric degradation to noospheric exaltation; the annual wavespell is governed by the same principle of pulsar organization as the 13-kin wavespell (see below).

II. Galactic Fourth-Dimensional Cycle (260 kin)

13-Kin Wavespell: master galactic timing cycle for establishing fourth-dimensional order of reality; organized as four interactive pulsars which create the geometry of time, provides matrix of role-playing for establishing 'pulsar bombs', focalized telepathic target projects for establishing cosmic consciousness while eliminating toxic waste; organized into five 52-day castles of four wavespells each, each castle defines a fundamental tone and rhythm of the fifth force order of galactic consciousness; 20 wavespells per 260-kin spin, 28 wavespells per 13-moon year.

20-Kin Harmonic Run: master organizer for the Planet Art work rhythms; based upon teams of planetary kin operating according to their galactic signatures, each galactic signature has multiple functions within the 20-kin harmonic run determined by four different orders of organization; there are 13 harmonic runs per galactic spin; within any harmonic run, Dragon to Sun, by solar seal of the galactic signature, any planetary kin participates in the four orders at one phase or another within the 20-kin harmonic run.

1) *Clans: environmental affairs.* The four Clans run in five-kin chromatic units each coded by the four master colors — yellow fire, red blood, white truth and blue sky; during your five-kin run you are responsible for developing that phase of environmental biospheric order.

2) *Time Cells: artistic affairs.* Five Time Cells of four kin each are organized as a coherent informational cycle — input, store, process, output, matrix; depending upon the location of your galactic signature you participate in one of these five Time Cells and are responsible for helping to administer that phase of the 20-kin art process.

3) *Earth Family, domestic affairs.* The 20 tribes of time are organized as five Earth Families: every five kin, one's Earth Family occurs within the 20-kin harmonic run; these govern the kin when you participate in domestic affairs — cooking, cleaning house, etc.

4) *Color Family: master coordination.* Each galactic signature belongs to one of four color groups: red initiates, white refines, blue transforms, yellow ripens; by color determination every four days you participate in the master coordination of the social process, crossing over concerns of the Clans, Time Cells and Earth Families. In this way the Color Family represents a fourth-dimensional fulfillment of the Rainbow Nation.

Pursuing these models, the planetary kin will create a galactic lottery for assignment of new roles as planetary kin and help

establish a level of unprecedented social and sexual equality.
20 fingers and toes: body is the instrument of the living solar mind.
28 days, the biological cycle of the moon, to live one lunar life.
One solar mind, one lunar life
make one planetary kin living in galactic time.

The Japanese model: the new dispensation and the transformation of the human planetary organism

All that is required to implement bioregionally the new order of 'time is art' is the example of one cultural bioregion collectively determining to shift its will and priorities from industrial production to artistic organization. The cultural bioregion most prepared to make this kind of rapid and unprecedented shift seems to be Japan.

Within its island bioregion, Japanese culture represents a human transformer enzyme. Through the various transformative phases of its history, it has maintained an unparalleled level of spiritual, artistic and social sophistication. Its most recent transformation followed the singular, devastating impact of two atomic weapons dropped on the cities of Hiroshima and Nagasaki, August 6 and 9, 1945. From an industrialized Samurai war culture, in two generations the Japanese became the world leader in technological innovation.

It is important to bear in mind that these two generations were also two generations of peace in which the Japanese experienced no internal conflict, nor did they develop any external military force, and hence have not engaged in global military adventures of any kind. It is Japan's unparalleled economic and technological prowess that earned its entry as the only Asian member of the G-7. While Japan has advanced to the pinnacles of third-dimensional materialism, its basic culture of peace has ensured that at its root is a profoundly spiritual culture.

At the highest corporate levels, as well as throughout the youth culture, there is an impending sense that the current process of materialism can go no farther and that a new direction must be sought. The 13-Moon Calendar Change Peace Movement, though small in numbers, has skillfully penetrated many levels of popular culture through mass media forms, especially youth magazines and *manga*, the popular form of comic book.

Dating from September 2, 1945, and paralleling the 50-year culture of peace maintained by the Japanese people, has been the growth of an astonishing movement and way of life known as *Rinri*, ethical enlightenment. The *Rinri* movement numbers in the millions. *Rinri* leadership has been contacted and has demonstrated receptivity to the 13-Moon Calendar Change Peace Movement.

The moment is right for a full-scale galactic cultural revolution to occur in Japan, transforming Japanese culture into the model of the collective human planetary organism operating according to the new dispensation of time. This can be rapidly and peacefully accomplished by engaging the finest and best of the current technologies and mass media, in accord with high level planning councils of corporate and spiritual leaders. The point is to agree on the need to shift the economic priorities from biospheric waste to artistic regeneration, the creation of a galactic, telepathic technology and to begin to take immediate action.

By placing the biospheric whole and biospheric rights as a goal above and beyond national ego and industrial profit, Japanese culture would model and enact the principles of biospheric *Rinri*. The wealth and energy of the current economy would be converted into the up-scaling of the enormous artistic and spiritual resources of the people. Thrusting Japan on the world stage, this time as a model of the galactic culture of peace, could have a thoroughly cathartic and inspiring effect on many other peoples and cultures of the planet.

Granting of Biospheric Amnesty

By replacing the current anachronistic and irregular 12-month calendar with the harmonic and biologically accurate 13-moon, 28-day calendar, humanity is preparing a new covenant for itself. The covenant based on the new time of 13 moons may be provisionally known as the 'Covenant of Biospheric Rights'.

The time has come to recognize that as a species we humans form an interdependent link within a larger, living whole, the biosphere of planet Earth. With the adoption of the biologically correct calendar which places us in harmony again with the biosphere and the larger cycles of nature, we humans accept that our rights are not created by man-made laws, but are determined and granted by the biosphere. Biospheric Amnesty is granted and effective through the date Crystal Moon 28, June 26, 1996, '13-Moon Victory Day'.

A small but critical number of humans have already adopted and entered the new calendar of 13 moons. In order to ensure a peaceful and orderly transition from the false 12:60 time to the correct 13:20 time, biospheric amnesty is granted to all existing human institutions in order that their leaders and constituents may have the time and opportunity to grasp the implications of changing the calendar and to prepare for reorganization according to the biospheric standards of the new time.

It is important to bear in mind that from the point of view of the planetary biosphere, it is the continuing entrainment of human life and civilization in the 12:60 timing frequency that is systematically disrupting and destroying the biosphere — humanity's life-support system. In order to avoid an act of collective planetary suicide, the Pax Cultura Pax Biospherica is invoked.

Further, in recognition that the present condition of humanity is dominated and governed by an industrial bankers' alliance known as the G-7, specific appeal is made to the leaders, finance ministers, bank and corporate executives of the G-7 to receive this summons and seriously consider that, from the biospheric perspective, their options are now closed down and their reign of power is ended. Biospheric Amnesty offers the G-7, and its interwoven ally the Euro-12, an honorable and dignified way in which to understand that a creative exit from the old order of time is still fully possible.

From 'Japan' Document, September 1995

THIRTEEN

Practicing the Universal Equality of Awareness

The fundamental technique for cultivating the state of nowness is referred to as 'practicing the universal equality of awareness'. This is the only way to maintain genuine freshness of mind. Without this freshness of mind, the conditionings of the 12:60 timing frequency will continue to occlude clear seeing and the capacity for extended sensory vision or fourth-dimensional insight. In these two capacities of mind, clear seeing and extended sensory vision, are the two goals of practicing the universal equality of awareness.

This practice is called universal because it can be undertaken by any human, and its object of experience is the universal nature of mind which is nothing more than the uncategorized equality of all phenomena and experiences with each other. The experience of universal equality is maintained by an awareness that is actually constant or constantly available in the moment by bringing your mind back to it. Practice of the universal equality of awareness brings about a mind that is without judgement yet discriminating, calm yet vigilant, and receptive to synchronic nuances of sensory mental input — extended sensory vision, which is the root of telepathic fourth-dimensional knowing and experience. All of these qualities of mind are in the now, and free of third-dimensional conceptual clinging.

To practice universal equality of awareness, first understand the nature of mind, then the nature of mind as it has been conditioned by the 12:60 timing frequency.

The nature of mind is unobstructed clarity contaminated by neither content nor goal; its energetic capacity is to appreciate and spontaneously formulate sensory input into catalytic imagery capable of being communicated and/or translated into bodily movement or action. If the mind remains fresh and open, bodily movement and action remain spontaneous and free. Self-esteem is the spiritual root of the body moving in time. Without self-esteem there is no patience to watch the mind; without watching and knowing the mind, the body will not be able to move freely in time.

Immersed in and conditioned by the 12:60 timing frequency, the mind loses its inherent freshness; its spontaneity is drastically reduced, becoming constantly ego-specific in its orientation, goal-oriented in its referencing, and clock-dependent in its governance. Not knowing any other way, these attributes of mind become second nature, collectively creating the 12:60 mental field called materialism. Materialism is mental addiction to a belief in the exclusive power of third-dimensional physical plane reality. The root of materialism as a state of mind is conditioned by the regimen of the seven-day week.

Even though 52 weeks follow in perfect regularity, the irregular reckoning of the 12-month calendar is not in accord with the seven-day week. For this reason, the days of the week and the days of the month are continuously different and random, month after month, year after year. This conditions the 12:60 mind to egoic shortsightedness on behalf of the attainment of its own survival goals, and amnesia about all else.

The coherent capacity of the mind to entrain a cyclic comprehension of no more than a generic week is further reinforced by money, which is rewarded for the time one has given to a job during five days of the week. In this way the week becomes the measure of time allotted to 'earn one's bread', while the weekend becomes the primary and all-consuming goal or escape-valve. The shut-down this creates to the original unobstructed condition of mind is profound; but when the clock is thrown in as the instrument for regulating one's bodily momentum, then the situation of the 12:60 timing frequency becomes totally unnatural and unhealthy.

The inherent problem of the clock is the profound lack of trust it engenders in the body's own inherent timing frequency. The arbitrary division of the day — one kin — into 24 hours, each hour into 60 minutes, each minute into 60 seconds, and each second, by means of cesium atomic clocks, reducible to infinitesimal portions of itself, all of this factored into an endless, random, unpatterned relationship of months to days of the week, results in a mental situation of chaotic simultaneity and entropic solutionlessness.

Even humans who practice some form of meditation, mental awareness training, or prayer and spiritual service inevitably succumb to the grinding ceaselessness of the clock-fueled state of consciousness known as 12:60 materialism. It is for this reason that the practice of universal awareness of equality becomes mandatory in order to release oneself from the conditions of the 12:60 and to entrain the mind in the 13:20 frequency.

The first step is to cultivate clear seeing. Since mind is originally unobstructed clarity of awareness, and since, in truth, the equality of this awareness never ceases, no matter how much 12:60 conceptualization is generated as second-nature reality, one has only to understand this: no matter what its content, any thought or conceptualization experienced by the mind is self-generated and devoid of any real substance, a mere electroneural flash and nothing more.

By sitting still and holding the spine erect yet relaxed, watch the flow of thoughts. By watching the flow of thoughts one can see that in actuality no thought is more or less important than any other; it is only different ego attachments that make them seem so. Seeing the current of thoughts in this way one can experience the universal equality of awareness as the flow of thoughts undifferentiated by egoic evaluation. By doing this for a few moments at a time, and extending it as one becomes more familiar with the practice, one can come to distinguish that there is actually 'space' between thoughts. This space between thoughts is the original unobstructed nature of mind. Through further practice one can extend oneself for longer periods into this non-conceptualized space. To experience this space is to taste the essence of nowness. In the space of now there is no history, no 12:60, no ego, no beginning and no end. Because one learns to see without concepts, cultivating this space is called cultivating clear seeing.

Within the space of nowness, time continuously arises. Awareness of the time within the non-conceptual space is referred to as panoramic awareness. Panoramic awareness is the universal equality of mind attentive to the total experience of the body and mind as a unified movement in time. Sitting still in panoramic awareness, and entering freely without goal into the qualities of sensory experience which spontaneously occur, is called cultivating extended sensory vision. It is through cultivating extended sensory vision that genuine insight may arise.

This insight, occurring in the space of nowness between and even within thoughts, is referred to as synchronic insight, for it is a result not of a belabored, conditioned process of 12:60 mental rationalization, but of a simultaneous fusion of sensory-psychic input given comprehension through time. Growing out of a familiarity with extended sensory vision, synchronic insight is the basis of the realization of divinatory intelligence, the direct form of knowing necessary for the practice of chronomancy. All divination is direct application of intelligence.

Intelligence is the other attribute of mind which balances awareness. Both awareness and intelligence are factors of resonance permeating all constructs of reality. While awareness, clear seeing and the cultivation of synchronic insight is rooted in mental attentiveness to sensory input (including its own), intelligence refers to the resonant strata of time which order the synchronic manifestation of phenomena.

In nature the resonant strata of time are the schedule of frequencies by which coherence is maintained in the phenomenal world, the world perceptible to the senses. Within the mind, resonant strata of time refers to the schedule of frequencies by which psychic coherence is maintained, and the different orders of psychic information are made available, inclusive of their means of communication, i.e. telepathy. Relieved of the burdens of having to maintain the artificial mental order of the 12:60 consciousness, the mind releases itself easily into its own intelligence. Knowing is innate. Experience transcends further instruction.

Finally, universal equality of awareness is maintained through attention to breath. Whether while sitting with spine erect or at any time of the waking life, if the distraction of 12:60 mental rationalizations becomes overwhelming, it is easy to wake up, take note and return to the breath. In other words, let the complex conceptualization be released with the exhalation, and with the new inhalation let there be clear mind of nowness. Since the respiration of the human corpus represents the other end of the CO_2 cycle generated by plant photosynthesis, the human intelligence brought consciously to bear on the breath results in a restoration of universal equality of awareness within the CO_2 cycle itself. In this way, practiced and understood by growing numbers of the human corpus, universal equality of awareness becomes the basis of a galactic culture. Galactic culture is culture free of all historical, culturally limiting chauvinisms, opening instead to the life of universal equality of all kin.

From *A Treatise on Time Viewed from Its Own Dimension*

A Note on Group Work

Start forming into small groups. To generate the energy, work in groups of three — form triangles. In any group of 12 there are four main groups of three. It doesn't matter who the people are. We are dealing in humans, not in roles people play. It is the human-to-human energy hookups within the triangles that are important. And remember that you can work in as many triangles as you need to. Every group of 12 becomes a node. The purpose is to generate energy and to link up with other twelves: for all group nodes to be linked up as a collective. When this starts to happen, you are creating a Crystal Earth energy grid which envelopes the planet. Get your circles turning, and be ready to go, because, when the value goes out of money, and the Earth starts talking heavy weather, these groups need to be in place.

To keep in touch with the latest news and developments, including regular updates from José Argüelles, see VictoryNet Website at
http://www.victory-net.com/
It is also possible to join the VictoryNet Round Table — see Resources section at end of book.

The Banner of Peace

Time, the g-force, webs our cells to each passing day.
The webbing of a day is called a kin.
The body is kin; it is what time webs.
Each body is kin to every other body.
The Earth is the medium which g-force uses
to web each body to every other body,
kin after kin, spin after spin.

My body is kin to all other kin.
The dog is kin as are the trees,
and every stone and blade of grass is webbed to me as kin.
Multiple and numberless are my kin.
Webbed, renewed at every moon
and recycled every solar spin,
breathed as time, galactic web.
Each dawn marries me
to my infinite and ceaseless round of kin.

Recorded at the Inn of the Mayan Cycles
8 Storm, Electric 5, Blue Cosmic Storm Year
(AD 1992)

José Argüelles

José Argüelles (born 1939), planetary whole systems anthropologist, received his Ph.D. in Art History and Aesthetics from the University of Chicago in 1969. In a distinguished career as an educator, he taught at Princeton University, University of California, Evergreen State College, San Francisco State University, San Francisco Institute of Art, the Naropa Institute, the University of Colorado, and the Union Graduate School.

His pioneering books resulting from investigations into human whole systems include: *Mandala* (1972), *A Psychophysical Aesthetic* (1972), *The Transformative Vision: Reflections on the Nature and History of Human Expression* (1975, 1992), *Surfers of the Zuvuya* (1989), *The Arcturus Probe* (1992) and most importantly *Earth Ascending: An Illustrated Treatise on the Law Governing Whole Systems* (1984, 1988).

As one of the founders of Earth Day (First Whole Earth Festival, Davis, California, 1970), Argüelles is a career activist for peace and the planetary transformation of consciousness. He and his wife and partner, Lloydine, founded the Planet Art Network (1983), promoting the revival of the Nicholas Roerich Peace Pact and Banner of Peace (1935). Combining investigations of the Roerich Peace Pact with his lifetime study of the mathematics and prophecies of the Mayan calendar, Argüelles initiated the Harmonic Convergence, August 16-17 1987, global meditation and planetary peace event.

Following his unraveling of the Mayan calendar code in his international bestseller, *The Mayan Factor: Path Beyond Technology* (1987), Argüelles, with his wife, continued his scientific and mathematical investigations of the timing frequency underlying the Mayan calendar system of ancient Central America. The result of their research was the discovery of the 12:60—13:20 timing frequencies and the breakthrough set of tools and proofs of the mathematics of the fourth-dimensional time, *Dreamspell: The Journey of Timeship Earth 2013* (1991, 1992), the *13-Moon Calendar* (1992), *A Treatise on Time Viewed from Its Own Dimension* (1992), and finally *Telektonon: the Talking Stone of Prophecy*, the 13-moon calendar, prophecy, game and universal peace plan (1993-94).

VICTORYNET
The Planetary Rainbow Tribe Networking Guide

OPERATION VICTORY
is dedicated to coordinating the advancement of the Oneness of Humanity and Planetary Transformation

THE GALACTIC CULTURAL STRATEGY

A curriculum instituted by Planetary Calendar Council groups to activate the Rainbow Tribe. Time is the basis of culture; below are the tools for understanding Galactic Time.

1) Dreamspell Calendar of Planetary Service, 13-Moon 28-Day
PM 5   Black and white wall calendar $10.00*
PM 5a   Full color pocket calendar $13.00*
This takes us to the first stage of galactic knowledge where we learn the difference between the false Gregorian 12:60 time and the true galactic 13:20 time, reconnecting us to our natural rhythms.

2) Telektonon, Game of Prophecy

PM 10 . . . .$39.00*

As we increase the numbers of humanity who follow the 13-Moon Calendar, we increase the general bio-telepathic field of resonance. This Telektonon playing board is the sword of light, the technology of telepathy.

3) Telektonon, Teaching Video

VT 12 . . . .$29.95*

A comprehensive introductory video to help you with the game.

4) Dreamspell, The Journey of Timeship Earth 2013 Kit

PM 9 . . . .$39.00*

While the 13-Moon Calendar and the Telektonon fulfill the purpose of biologically and telepathically restoring the human to its rightful role and place within the planetary biosphere, it is the Dreamspell which provides the social reorganizing factor of the new time, the operating tools for navigating fourth-dimensional time.

5) Dreamspell, Teaching Video, by José & Lloydine Argüelles

VT 11 . . . .$29.95*

A comprehensive introductory video to help you with the kit.

6) Moons in Motion, Turtle of the 13 Moons, 26-page booklet

PM 12 . . . .$6.00

A Dreamspell primer written by José Argüelles.

7) Treatise on Time, book by José Argüelles

PM 11 . . . .$11.95

A complete description of the discovery of the 12:60—13:20 timing frequencies and of the mathematical laws governing the radial matrix of fourth-dimensional time.

8) Dreamspell, Calendar Software

IBM   PM7 . . . .$13.00
Macintosh PM8 . . . .$13.00

With this software you find your galactic signature and place in the Rainbow Tribe. You will also find the meditation of the day.

* Wholesale: 40% discount for 12 items or more, plus shipping.

EXTRATERRESTRIAL AND HUMAN EVOLUTION LECTURE SERIES
First Lecture Series (1993-4): Extraterrestrial Contact and Human Evolution

Lecture #1 (Dec 2, 1993)
General Overview and Update
• The Galactic Federation • The Genesis story • Lemuria and Atlantis
• Earth changes • The coming mass landings • Photon Belt • Transformation/Ascension process

A1 for 2-hour audio tapes, **A2** for 2-hour video tape

Lecture #2 (Dec 9, 1993)
First Contact — Its Meaning and Implications
• Mass landings • The role of the Federation • The role of cetaceans •
Preparing for the Photon Belt • New Technology, New Psychology •
Lady Gaia and Earth changes

A2 for 2-hour audio tapes, **V2** for 2-hour video tape

Lecture #3 (Dec 30, 1993)
New Bodies and Full Consciousness
• Photon Belt phenomenon • New chakra system • Talking with the
rocks, plants and animals • Ascension process • Integration of changes
• Angelic hierarchy

A3 for 2-hour audio tapes, **V3** for 2-hour video tape

Lecture #4 (Jan 6, 1994)
The Return of the Lyran/Sirian Culture
• The laws of relationships • Spiritual sexuality • The role of counselors
• The Clans • Cultural practices and traditions • The Sirian councils

A4 for 2-hour audio tapes, **V4** for 2-hour video tape

Lecture #5 (Feb 25, 1994)
Earth Spiritual Hierarchy and the Galactic Federation
• What is the Spiritual Hierarchy? • Their involvement with the Galactic Federation • The roles of archangels, angels, Ascended Masters and
devas • Role of Spiritual Hierarchy in Ascension process • Earth/
human transformation • The coming mass landings • The Second Coming and the Photon Belt • Our holographic envelope

A5 for 2-hour audio tapes, **V5** for 2-hour video tape

Lecture #6 (March 11, 1994)

Linking the Hawaiians, the Mayans and the Tibetans

● Role of Lemuria today and tomorrow ● Mass migrations after its destruction ● The legacy of the Lemurian culture: Hawaii, Tibet and Mexico ● Galactic influence ● Religious concept of time ● Mayan and Tibetan cultural links ● Magic of Hawaii ● Reflection on three remnant cultures of Lemuria

A6 for 2-hour audio tapes, **V6** for 2-hour video tape

Lecture #7 (March 25, 1994)

Our Ascension/Transformation Process

● What is Ascension? ● Different levels of consciousness ● Role of angelic hierarchy in Ascension ● How to prepare for Ascension ● Integrating the changes in your consciousness ● How consciousness affects our genetics ● Photon Belt and the new galactic civilization

A7 for 2-hour audio tapes, **V7** for 2-hour video tape

Lecture #8 (April 29, 1994)

Cetaceans and the Spiritual Hierarchy

● Update on cetacean (dolphin and whale) contact ● Preparing for human guardianship ● The interaction of the cetaceans and the Spiritual Hierarchy ● Defining human guardianship ● Cetaceans as teachers of galactic wisdom ● The Spiritual Hierarchy's role in planetary guardianship

A8 for 2-hour audio tapes, **V8** for 2-hour video tape

Lecture #9 (June 10, 1994)

Planetary Advocate Groups — Guidelines

This is useful information for those interested in establishing a Planetary Advocate Group.

● What is a Planetary Advocate Group? ● How to form a Planetary Advocate Group ● How to be an advocate and liaison for planet Earth ● How the Planetary Advocate Groups relate to the Spiritual Hierarchy and the Galactic Federation ● The role of Planetary Advocate Groups in creating the emerging web of planetary consciousness ● The role of Planetary Advocate Groups before and after the mass landings ● Planetary Advocate Groups and the new galactic civilization

A9 for 2-hour audio tapes, **V9** for 2-hour video tape

Lecture #10 (August 17, 1994)
When Are You Becoming a Galactic Human?
You may have heard him before but you haven't heard this one.
● How to prepare for the coming Earth changes ● Updates on integrating your light body and your physical body ● Updates on your new consciousness and its effects on this planet ● Update on the Photon Belt and the new galactic civilization ● The importance of Planetary Advocate Groups and how to create them

A10 for 2-hour audio tapes, **V10** for 2-hour video tape

Lecture #11 (August 17, 1994)
The Four Laws and an Update on First Contact
This is very interesting and packed with current information.
● The Four Galactic Human Laws explained ● Applications of the Laws for contemporary society ● Earth human protocols for first contact ● Starship identification and landing procedures ● Angelic Hierarchy procedures for the mass landing ● Information about the Golden Age coming in December

A11 for 2-hour audio tapes, **V11** for 2-hour video tape

Lecture #12 (Sept 22, 1994)
Why is Earth Becoming a Galactic Planet?
● The complete Crystal Earth transformation cycle ● How you can prepare for the coming changes on planet Earth ● Updates on how these Earth changes will affect the mass landing scenario ● Updates on how the Earth's changes will influence the entire solar system ● Update on the spiritual and physical changes affecting everyone ● Why the changes on Earth are important to our transformation/ascension

A12 for 2-hour audio tapes, **V12** for 2-hour video tape

Lecture #13 (Oct 13, 1994 & Nov 21, 1994)
Crystal Earth: Its Cosmic Destiny
This is even better.
● Messages on the landings from Lords Metatron and Michael ● How the Solar System will be restored by the year 2013 ● The latest on the exiting of the dark energy in South America ● A report on the Intergalactic Truce ● New information on the crystalline Earth ● An update from the Galactic Federation's First Contact Team ● Startling data on your Transformation/Ascension process

A13 for 2-hour audio tapes (Original lecture, Oct 13 1994, in Mountain

View. Includes Miriam Nidle's farewell speech and final appearance).
V13 for **1-hour** video tape (Lecture only, recorded November 21, 1994 in a studio), SPECIAL @ $25.00

Lecture #14 (December 6, 1994)
A Surprising Collection of Lost Information
Completely new and startling information with commentaries by Peggy McConnell.
• The real story and origins of Jesus the Christ • The legends and history of the Buddha • The connections between ancient Egypt, Atlantis and us • Earth grids and human meridians — a connection in consciousness • Operation protocols and the mass landings • Revelations, ascension and transformation: an update • The coming year and a revised paradigm for a new golden age

A14 for 2-hour audio tapes, **V14** for 2-hour video tape

SECOND LECTURE SERIES (1995): CRYSTALLINE EARTH AND YOUR TRANSFORMATION

Lecture #1 (Feb 23, 1995)
The Evolving Destiny of Earth's Humanity
• The revised mass landing scenario • The Sirians then and now • New twist on galactic time • A critical message from Lord Michael and Lord Metatron • Latest changes in our spiritual and physical bodies • The Truce of Anchara and peace with Dinoids/Reptoids • How our transformation will affect life in the Galaxy • Status of our transformation/ascension

A2-1 for 2-hour audio tapes, **V2-1** for 2-hour video tape

Lecture #2 (May 18, 1995)
The Divine Intervention Begins
• The landings in Mexico: their importance • A new and changing role for the Galactic Federation • A plan to establish the new Life/Light centers • A new definition for consciousness • A report from the First Contact Team • The status and importance of the Galactic Truce

A2-2 for 2-hour audio tapes, **V2-2** for 2-hour video tape

Lecture #3 (June 22, 1995)
The Reality of Full Consciousness
• Exploring the Ascension/Transformation process • The true nature of full consciousness • A new definition of life • Life and its relationship to the soul • The soul, your life and the Spiritual Hierarchy • Angels, Guardians and Earth Spirits • The new Earth grids and our responsibilities • Our galactic civilization: a scenario

A2-3 for 2-hour audio tapes, **V2-3** for 2-hour video tape

Lecture #4 (July 20, 1995)
The Unknown Reasons for Full Consciousness
• The ascension/transformation process and humanity • The crystalline Earth and our transformation • A new explanation of ascension • Life and the key role for consciousness • The Spiritual Hierarchy: a new reality for humanity • The history behind Earth's cosmic destiny

A2-4 for 2-hour audio tapes, **V2-4** for 2-hour video tape

Lecture #5 (August 18, 1995)
The Crystalline Earth and Our Galaxy
• Our Earth as an interdimensional being • The significance of our galaxy to the creation • Mass landings on Earth as a fulfillment of prophecy • The reasons for the interdimensional holograms • Why we are in the midst of galactic change • The Earth and our chakras • Light and darkness and its role in creation • Life, wisdom and the sixth creation: a brief discourse

A2-5 for two 90-minute audio tapes, **V2-5** for 2-hour video tape

Lecture #6 (September 28, 1995)
Earth's Humanity: Its Cosmic Destiny
• The implications of a galactic society • The dramatic changes for the coming year • The Galactic Federation and humanity — a perspective • Our Ascension process: the whys and hows • Earth and our civilization — new realities • Life: an amazing expression of new perceptions • This Creation: a brief history • Mass landings: new information, new scenario

A2-6 for two 90-minute audio tapes, **V2-6** for 2-hour video tape

Lecture #7 (Nov 9, 1955)
The Sixth Creation and Prophecy
• Our galaxy and the Earth — a perspective • The galaxy and its place

in the Sixth Creation ● Messages from Lord Michael and Lord Metatron ● The mass landings and their place in a new prophecy ● The celestial time table as adjusted for our solar system ● Full consciousness and the new science

A2-7 for 2-hour audio tapes, **V2-7** for 2-hour video tape

Other Information

'Galactic Time' Workshop — videos and booklet
Based on the Mayan calendar and José Argüelles's Dreamspell Game. Understanding Galactic Time will be useful in the new galactic civilization that is emerging.
● 20 Sacred Glyphs ● 13 Tones of Creation ● Wavespells and Castles ● Tzolkin ● Haab

VT5 for a 4-hour video & 18-page booklet @ $50

'Becoming a Galactic Human' Workshop — video only
This workshop presents what it means to become a galactic human along with an in-depth look at Fluid Management leadership principles and the Ral-Ba meditation technique.
● What it means to be a galactic human ● Theory and practice of fluid management ● Exploring group consciousness ● Fluid management exercises ● Ral-Ba: a new meditation to anchor the higher frequencies ● A method to empower and rejuvenate the mind ● Nature of the new realignments of the chakras ● How to better adjust your light body to the new chakras

VT7 for a 4-hour video @ $50.00

The Day Out of Time — video only
José and Lloydine Argüelles
Watching this video allows you to participate in one of the most powerful ceremonies at the end of this 26,000-year Mayan Cycle. Sunrise, midday and sunset ceremonies of a planetary rainbow gathering at Serpent Mount, Ohio, on July 25, 1995, A Day Out of Time. Interviews with José and Lloydine Argüelles on the Mayan Calendar.

VT13 for a 104-minute video @ $29.95

Sheldon Nidle Answers Questions Regarding the Photon Belt and Mass Landings (May 17, 1995)
(30 minutes — audio only)
Sheldon answers commonly asked questions regarding these topics.

QA1 for a 30-min. audio tape @ $7; S&H = $4 for Priority Mail & $1 each additional.

Printed Materials

PM3A Galactic Human Handbook / Entering the New Time and Creating Planetary Groups $11.95
PM12 The Mayan Factor, The Path Beyond Technology *by José Argüelles* $12.95
PM13   Surfers of the Zuvuya: Tales of Interdimensional Travel *by José Argüelles* $15.00

Ordering

US orders: See Order Form. Send order to:

> **Operation Victory USA**
> 1450 4th Street, Suite 6
> Berkeley, CA 94710
> USA
> Tel +1 (510) 559-8102, Fax +1 (510) 559-9493

For audio and video tapes, add 8.25% California tax plus shipping and handling charges. For printed materials add shipping and handling charges. Foreign orders multiply shipping by 3 (or order from regional centers — see over).

Wholesale: 40% discount for 12 items or more, plus shipping

SHIPPING AND HANDLING CHARGES		
Subtotal	US	Canada
Up to $20.00	Add $4.00	Add $5.00
$20.01-$40.00	$5.00	$6.00
$40.01-$60.00	$6.00	$7.00
$60.01-$80.00	$8.00	$10.00
In US and Canada, shipping is UPS ground or equivalent. For rush shipping call (510) 559-8102 or Fax (510) 559 9493		

Outside USA: to find out regional prices and shipping and handling charges, contact your regional center:

Operation Victory Europe
Parkmount House
10 St Leonards Road
Forres IV36 0DW, Scotland
Tel/Fax +44 01309 673312

Operation Victory Australia
40 George Street
North Hobart, Tasmania 7000
Australia
Tel +61 02 346687
Fax +61 02 312578

Operation Victory New Zealand
PO Box 66-067
Beach Haven
Auckland 1310
New Zealand
Tel/Fax +64 9 483 5174

OPERATION VICTORY
GENERAL ORDER FORM
(To be detached or photocopied)

Name _____

Address _____

_____ City _____

State/Country _____ Zip/Post Code _____

Phone (optional) _____

QUANTITY	PRICE	DESCRIPTION	AMOUNT
_____	_____	_____	_____
_____	_____	_____	_____
_____	_____	_____	_____
_____	_____	_____	_____
_____	_____	_____	_____
_____	_____	_____	_____
_____	_____	_____	_____
_____	_____	_____	_____
_____	_____	_____	_____

Please check if first order ☐

Date _____   Total _____

       * Shipping and handling _____

(For California residents) 8.25% Sales Tax _____

      Grand Total _____

☐ Cash   ☐ Money Order   ☐ Check

☐ Mastercard/Visa no:

_____

Expiry date _____ Signature _____

Thank you for your order

Send with payment to your regional distribution point

VICTORYNET ROUND TABLE

- Round Table will connect you worldwide with lightworkers and planetary groups
- Round Table will supply the most current information from around the globe
- Round Table will keep you up to date about spiritual events
- Round Table will synchronize and coordinate our efforts to shift the mass consciousness

Get online with a local Internet provider and once you have your e-mail address, fill out the signup procedure below.

VICTORYNET ROUND TABLE SIGNUP PROCEDURE
(To be detached or photocopied)

Step 1: Complete the following:

Name _____

Address _____

City _____

State/Country _____ Zip/post code _____

User Name _____

Password (5 or more characters) _____

Step 2: Enclose the following:
US$84.00 yearly subscription

☐ Visa/Master Card   ☐ My check is enclosed

Visa/Master Card no. _____

Expiry date _____

Planetary Group Information
If you are a member of a Planetary Group, please complete the following information. As soon as your group has formed, please forward the following information to us and advise us of any changes. All groups and their locations will be posted in the guide.

Group name _____

Group function _____

continued over . . .

E-mail _____

Liaison name _____

Phone _____

Address _____

City _____

State/Country _____ Zip/post code _____

Mail to: Operation Victory, 1450 4th Street, Suite 6, Berkeley,
CA 94710, USA. Tel +1 (510) 559 8102, Fax +1 (510) 559 9493.

http://www.victory-net.com/

WEBSITES ON VICTORYNET

VictoryNet is the first planetary computer network dedicated to the advancement of the oneness of humanity and planetary transformation. VictoryNet is the place in space and time to tune in to the virtual community of consciousness (seminars, workshops, books, newsletters, products, etc) and all that is occurring on the planet to bring in the light.

We invite you to become part of the victory, the net and celebration of humanity. Listed below are the packages and rates to choose from for your own website within the VictoryNet, a living mandala.

Primary Resource Site Package

- An individual listing in the VictoryNet Resource Site Index, which appears by category on the VictoryNet home page. Your pages appear within VictoryNet. The guide header will appear on top of your pages. Your URL address will be:

  http://www.victory-net.com/your name

- Up to four pages of text and images, designed for easy readability. The first page gives you space to present your logo, an introductory paragraph, and two pages for your basic presentation, with up to 250 words on each page. The last page is for a bio or story about you, or the people who are part of your organization.

Two photos or images. We suggest you use one on your first page and the other on your bio page. This is VictoryNet's standard format. Yours may vary according to your needs.

Introductory Level Resource Page

This listing package includes one page with one graphic or logo, an introductory paragraph and up to 150 words of text.

How Can You List in VictoryNet?

It's easy. Just mail the application form with your payment for the composition charge, the posting charge (if applicable) and any extra charges.

Listing Rates

Take advantage of our special introductory offer which waives the entire first year's maintenance charges for both our four and one page resource packages.

Composition Charges
Primary four page package $485
Introductory one page package $175

Site Maintenance (Posting) Fees
Primary four page package $245/year
Introductory one page package $145/year
Additional pages $25/year

Additional Services
Extra images $20/scan, plus $20 setup
Text changes $40/hour, with $25 minimum
Hand-keys copy $40/hour
Copywriting and editing $50/hour
Graphic design $50/hour
Links to other sites $10 within VictoryNet
                                       $20 outside VictoryNet

Downloadable audio, video or text files:
$25 minimum for setup, plus $25/megabyte per year with a 1 megabyte minimum.

Call for information on our rates for video filming, digitizing and editing; speciality programming and hit list reports.

What You Need to Send Us . . .
Include your text and images on disk as described below:
● Send your text on a Windows, IBM or Macintosh formatted 3.5" diskette. Save your wordprocessed text in Text Format if possible (include line breaks). Please indicate which section of text belongs on each page. Also send a printed copy of your text.
● Photographs, logos, or other images digitized and saved to diskette.
● Images and photos for VictoryNet to scan should be good quality. Please send only professional quality graphics.

Any client-composed pages must be professionally done to our specifications. Please contact us for specifications and setup.

VICTORYNET WEBSITE APPLICATION FORM
(To be detached or photocopied)

CATEGORY

☐ Primary site package   ☐ Intro level page

☐ Text/images enclosed on disk & paper

☐ Text/graphics on paper only

Posting fee _____

Composition charge _____

Editing/other fees _____

Subtotal _____

Total _____

CREDIT CARD

☐ VISA   ☐ MasterCard

Account number _____

Expiry date _____

Charge authorization signature _____

Organization & contact person _____

_____

E-mail _____

Phone _____

Best time to call _____

Address _____

_____

City _____

State/Country _____ Zip/Post Code _____

Please make check payable to Operation Victory, 1450 4th Street,
Suite 6, Berkeley, CA 94170, USA.
Tel +1 (510) 559 8102, Fax +1 (510) 559 9493